EMBRACING

New Directions

Civility Imprint

It's A Resurrection

Betty Speaks

Foreword H.E Sir Clyde Rivers Royal name HRH
Okogyeman Kobina Amissah1

Civility Imprint

Published by: Brianna Johnson

Copyright 2021 by Betty Speaks

All rights reserved.

ISBN: 9798530704147

Scriptures quotations marked, unless otherwise indicated, are taken from the Holy Bible, the new international version, and the King James Version KJV of the Holy Bible.
Dr. Betty Speaks' Book titles may be purchased in bulk for Educational, Ministerial, Businesses, Fund-raising or Sales Promotional use.

For information, please e-mail

betty.speaks@gmail.com

www.bettyspeaks.com

Printed in
The United States of America

FOREWARD

Dr. Betty Speaks is truly a prolific pioneer voice of resurrection imprint, a new global paradigm of creating the new you. At some point in life, we all have to resurrect again. What Dr. Speaks has mastered is the ability to help you find yourself in whatever dimension of life you're in. She has brought to the table the component of civility imprint, and this is the way to make the world work for everyone, with component of kindness and respect for all of humanity. The mastery of one's self takes away all competition with others and allows you to empower all in their authentic gifting's. In this anthology, you will find the best authors in the land at motivating and building people to move to a higher level and resurrecting their dreams. The opportunity to work with a person of the caliber of Dr. Betty Speaks is a once in a lifetime opportunity and I'm truly grateful to be a part of this newly created paradigm by Dr. Speaks. The world will be a better place as a result of this book and the legendary authors in this book, whose stories will inspire and empower all. Learn and know your Civility Imprint.

- Sir Clyde Rivers Royal name HRH Okogyeman Kobina Amissah1

Leaders
EMBRACING
New Directions
Civility Imprint
It's A Resurrection

Betty Speaks

Foreword Sir Clyde Rivers Royal name HRH
Okogyeman Kobina Amissah1

Table Of Contents

Author's Notes

The co-authors share their stories, ideas, life strategies plus principles that will inspire and endow global leaders to show up every day and make encouraging Imprints. Wholeheartedly, the co-authors messages are forthright, yet powerful civil imprints for life. Imprints that shall propel a leaders everyday thought, every action and ultimately all leaders shall achieve both personal and professional resurrections towards new directions. Those that are in leadership positions will be motivated to reach beyond what is required of them as well as do something extraordinary to promote the Golden Rule and the Civility Imprint Act!

~Dr. Betty Speak

"I am an Imprint Leader"

Dr. Peggie Etheredge Johnson, RC, BA, MA, MEd, EdD

Dr. Peggie Etheredge Johnson was born and reared in Saluda, South Carolina and is married to Bishop Richard S. Johnson, Jr. and they celebrated 50 years of marriage in 2020. They are the parents of three sons, Richard L., Michael R., and Joshua S. Johnson, three daughters-in-love, LaTanya, Nina, and Teritla Johnson, grandparents of five adorable grandchildren: triplets, Richard G., Daniel A., and Samuel R. Johnson, two granddaughters, Nia Amarie, and Kendall Ashlyn Johnson.

A vessel chosen by God to be a prayer warrior during

her youth, Dr. Johnson experienced the understanding and fulfillment of this gift later in life through the love and teachings of many spiritual mothers. She gave her life to the Lord at an early age in her hometown of Saluda, SC and continues to serve Him until this day. Her favorite life verses are Philippians 4:13, Jeremiah 29:11-13, and Psalm 27. She considers her greatest achievement and purpose in life is all that God has taught her on her knees and in ministry that serves, delivers, and enables, children, women, and others to be all that God has called them to be in and through His Word for His Kingdom.

Currently, she is the First Lady of Cathedral of Faith Ministries in Irmo, SC and Charlotte, NC where her husband is the founder and pastor. Dr. Johnson has held various positions in the local church, diocese, and international level and is a licensed missionary.

Dr. Johnson currently continues community service by attending a weekly Bible Study for women with BSF and is the Lead Instructor of the weekly *Workplace Bible Studies* for women. She is Certified Life Coach, inspirational/motivational, and transformational teacher and speaker, seminar/workshop leader, curriculum developer, researcher, and facilitator of various workshops and topics that also include guest lecturer of various topics and is the creator of the Facebook Group, Supporting Your S.I.S. (Spiritual Immune System) where she is live weekly with guests to share biblical principles to remain spiritually healthy and well in multiple dimensions. Dr. Johnson is a serial entrepreneur and is the founder/owner of Kingdom Of Pearls, LLC.

Dr. Johnson graduated with honors from Riverside High School in Saluda, SC in the last segregated class of 1970. She is a graduate of Kenneth Shuler's School of Cosmetology and is a Licensed Cosmetologist. She attended Palmer College and Midlands Technical College, graduated from W.L. Bonner College with a B.A. degree in Biblical Studies, graduated from Columbia International University with a M.A. degree in Theological Studies, and a M.Ed. degree in Curriculum and Instruction. She graduated from Capella University with honors with a Doctor of Education degree in Curriculum and Instruction (D.Ed.). She holds the Professional Educator Certification in Bible Teaching in all levels from the Association of Christian Schools International (ASCI) and Site Facilitator Certification in *The Truth Project* from the International Institute for Christian School Educators (IICSE). She is a member of the Association for Supervision and Curriculum Development (ASCD), recipient of various awards including the iChange Nations Global Leadership Award.

Professionally Dr. Johnson retired from Columbia International University in 2013 where she was a full time faculty member in the College Of Education, a professor in the Prison Initiative Women's Correctional Institution in the College of Arts and Science, Supervisor of the graduate and undergraduate Cross-Culture Bible Teaching Practicum course to Belize, Central America, Director of Bible Clubs in Ministry Skills Development and Director of Bible Field Experience in the College of Education. Currently she is an Adjunct Faculty instructor and continues to teach the *Children In Poverty* course and guest lecturer in the College of Education at CIU, and Commencement speaker for the final graduating class at the Women's Prison Associate Of Arts Program.

Working with children and women is her greatest passion and love. She has been involved in many ministries alongside her husband for more than 48 years. She is co-founder of the Lea Project, a ministry of Cathedral of Faith that ministers to the needs of children in poverty, locally and globally. She and her husband have traveled on missions' and educational trips to Belize, Central America, South Africa, Sierra Leone, Israel, Jordan, Egypt, Italy, Germany, France, Turkey, Puerto Ricco, Panama, Jamaica, the Virgin Islands, and many other countries. They have led teams from their Church to the village of Barranco in Belize, Central America where they have adopted an elementary school, painted the exterior and interior of the school, established a school lunch program, sponsored children to attend a Christian Summer Youth Camp, high school, provided clothing, shoes, school supplies, and met other needs.

One of Dr. Johnson's paramount desires in life is to always be in the perfect will of God and continue serving God through local and Global Missions. She is passionate about her family, children, families in poverty, hurting and suffering women as well as suffering children of poverty globally. Her hobbies include, spending time with her awesome grandchildren, evangelism, researching, learning, and sharing dynamics of diverse cultures, reading, writing, sewing, teaching, and digital scrapbooking. Dr. Johnson is the owner and CEO of Kingdom Of Pearls, LLC and an Independent Mary Kay Consultant. She is the author of *Kingdom Of Pearls: Recovering The Wounded Heart* co-author of seven books, of which 4 are best sellers; *Soulful Prayers* vol. 1 and 2, *When CEOs Pray*, *Business Principles For The Beauty CEO*, *Women Creating Impact, Souled Out* vol. 2, and *Soulful Affirmations: 365 Days Of Positive Thoughts To Begin Your Day.*

You may follow Dr. Johnson on all social media platforms @Dr.Peggie
Website: www.mykingdompearls.com
Email: peggie.etheredge.johnson@gmail.com

Embracing The Resurrection of S.E.R.V.A.N.T. Leadership

By: Dr. Peggie Etheredge Johnson

"True leadership must be for the benefit of the followers, not to enrich the leader."

~John Maxwell

Regardless of the foundational beginning of a leader, their most important impactful feature is how well they end. The value of great leadership is not how well one begins their journey, but how well they finish and the significant impact of leaders they influenced and continued their legacy of influence. Whatever God is revealing and resurrecting in this hour is not new but was previously modeled by others who were impacted by the perfect leader found in the Holy Scriptures. The Servant Leadership model of Jesus the Christ is one that should be resurrection for current leaders to have an eternal legacy imprint on the lives of those who are in their circle of influence.

Resurrection is the resurgence or revitalization or restoring to life something that is no longer thriving or flourishing. Jesus the Christ introduced the world to servant leadership during His brief physical appearance in the Gospels. First, He modeled the importance of seeking the Father before choosing disciples and then powerfully models the principles of serving followers in the process of training. He was aware of their future purpose to accept His vision as their own and follow in His footprints to turn the world upside down. Through the power of His resurrection, they were able to resurrect the world and present the perfect plan of God for His people.

We are now faced with a world, whose worldview is increasingly becoming non-biblical. Therefore, many have embraced unbiblical leadership styles that in many instances are offensive, abusive, and lack positive energetic influence for lasting imprints. Based on this personal observation I find it necessary to revisit some of the basic principles of servant leadership that influenced Jesus' leadership style and was so miraculously effective.

Every life is endowed with diverse stages and phases. Each one should not be taken lightly but entered into with an image of legacy and an imprint that will remain long after the physical body has transitioned back to the dust. So often this thought is entertained during the golden period, when youthful mistakes have occurred, and midlife crisis are producing fruit in every dimension. The process of servant leadership is first following an influential leader to gain wisdom, knowledge, and understanding and then reproducing those principles in the lives of those assigned to your leadership.

Being a survivor of spiritual abuse, church, hurt, and wounding of the Spirit, I understand the value of biblical servant leadership in maintaining spiritual health and wellness and supporting a healthy spiritual immune system in preparation for fighting the good fight of faith in spiritual warfare.

S is Sacrifice Without Solitude – Matthew 14:13-16

In this valuable process the word SERVANT is shared to indicate what Jesus modeled through His Works and Words that are worth resurrecting and emulating as leaders today. The letter S in SERVANT represents sacrifices. Jesus changed His agenda on many occasions to accommodate the great needs of the people.

The art of sacrificing is the willingness to give up something especially for the sake of someone or something else for the purpose of helping others. It is a self-sacrificing act of forfeiting something precious to serve in a greater capacity that will change the course or destiny of others thereby disrupting their legacy. This is the resurrection of self-denial and yielding oneself to serve others without considering the loss of personal gratification in solitude, for the moral good in serving God through meeting the felt needs of humanity.

When Jesus heard it, He departed from there by boat to a deserted place by Himself. But when the multitudes heard it, they followed Him on foot from the cities. And when Jesus went out He saw a great multitude; and He was moved with compassion for them, and healed their sick. When it was evening, His disciples came to Him, saying, "This is a deserted place, and the hour is already late. Send the multitudes away, that they may go into the villages and buy themselves food." But Jesus said to them, "They do not need to go away. You give them something to eat." Matthew 14: 13-16 (NKJV)

John Maxwell says, "To add value to others, one must first value others." I will add, in doing so, the Creator is recognized as Supreme in His decision to entrust others to our leadership and care.

Jesus not only knew the immediate need, but He also had a plan to meet their needs right where they were. He also knew His legacy involved correcting the hearts of the disciples. Therefore, His was strategic in involving them in the process of considering the peoples' needs above their own. In so doing He empowered them to follow His model of serving instead of expecting to be served or sending people away because of personal insufficiency. Jesus challenged them to think outside of the shell in providing what the crowd lacked, food. This seemingly insignificant leadership strategy intentionally interrupted the disciples natural thought process of the value of people based on the heart of God.

On several occasions, Jesus needed physical and emotional rest, but during the process of finding a solitary place, secure from service and serving, He was interrupted by the essential needs of the people. During this time, Jesus was overwhelmed with compassion for the people because of their great necessities. He saw them as sheep without a shepherd and people without sufficient leaders. Jesus' love and concern were revealed in His response and the expectation is that His followers would embrace His model in meeting the needs of others. Jesus was resurrecting the leadership experiences of Moses, that the current leaders had misinterpreted, deviated from, and disputed among themselves. Jesus expended the necessary time to first discover the people's needs and then minister to them accordingly.

Jesus was aware and practiced the grand necessities of periodic solitude are required for physical, spiritual, and emotional renewal and restoration of every leader, there are instances when the imperative example of submitting to God's will include our immediate service to others. The faith of every leader is constantly challenged but also tested in regard to our priorities. Additionally, leaders are consistently reminded that the individual standing before us in dire need, just might be an angel in human form sent by God.

Are leaders able and ready to meet the challenge of sacrificing an opportunity for solitary refurbishing to sustain future generations? Future leaders must know that

Jesus provides the power to meet every need and therefore, nothing is impossible. Additionally, solitude will always be a personal heart desire and available when necessary, however, but the needs of people will always be God's first heart desire. People matter and are valuable to God.

"The best way a mentor can prepare another leader is to expose him or her to other great people." ~John Maxwell

E is Encourage Without Exposure – Matthew 17:1-3

Have you noticed a trend in leadership that excludes to process of exposing the next generation to other great leaders for the selfish reason of wanting to be the greatest leader their circle of influence is aware of?

On one occasion Jesus took His inner circle, Peter, James, and John with Him to the mountain of transfiguration where they were exposed to Jesus' transfiguration and Moses and Elijah. He not only wanted them to see Him in all of His glory, but He encouraged them through observing something they had never seen before, Jesus speaking with two of the greatest prophets who ever lived on the face of the earth. Even though they misunderstood this miraculous action, it provided a teachable moment for Jesus and the privileged disciples. This opportunity to be in the presence of such greatness left a lasting imprint on the face of the earth through their ministry.

The art of encouragement involves leadership that nurtures inspiration with courage, hope, and confidence in an effort to expose others to the greatness and wonders of God trough His people.

"Everything rises and falls on leadership." ~John Maxwell

R is Relationship Without Repulsiveness – Luke 17:1-4

The art of engaging in authentic transparent relationships without the repulsive behavior of offending others intentionally is essential to servant leadership. Although difficult, Jesus warns the disciples how they must treat one another regarding offenses and the serious nature of the one guilty of such an offense. He declares the jeopardy of the one who offends and the offended who rebukes the offender.

Servant leaders are not push overs and do not place themselves in a position to be taken advantage of due to the misrepresentation of the Scriptures. Jesus clearly includes the use of rebuke for those who sin against their brother or sister. He indicates in these verses that in some instances, forgiveness is conditional and based on not when, but "if" the offender repents. This principle desperately needs resurrection for the prevention of limiting beliefs that leaders are commanded to forgive any and everyone at all times regardless of their attitudes and actions. Thereby, aiding in the development of healthy relationships.

"Ideas have a short shelf life. You must act on them before the expiration date. ~John Maxwell

V is Vision Without Violating – Matthew 22:37-40

Servant leaders are visionaries who present God's vision without violating His ancient commands for loving and keeping God first, while loving others as ourselves. Jesus used ancient wisdom to cast a new vision for the new covenant that introduces the new Kingdom, His Church, without violating the basic principles of the Holy Scriptures. How then is it that leaders are changing the meaning and written Word?

Sharing the vision is not sharing ideas, but revealing God's plans, goals, and will for His people throughout eternity. This is all about God and nothing about the leader, who is simply a vessel to inspire others to complete the legacy assignment of Jesus valiantly and vigorously without devaluing the significance of His Word.

"A leader is one who knows the way, goes the way, and shows the way." ~John Maxwell

A is Advocate Without Aggression – Matthew 5:38-42

The art of being an Advocate is to publicly support, protect, or endorse a particular cause or policy without being an aggressor. Jesus was a proponent of non-violence and taught this to His disciples and followers. He could have called an army to fight His battles and prevent Him from enduring the pain of the cross. However, He chose to do what He taught. Although He was an advocate for the unfortunate, and against injustice, He did so according to the will of His Father. He said what He said and did what He did without being quarrelsome, hostile, or belligerent. He spoke Truth and His anger was sinless.

"Leadership is influence." John Maxwell

N is Negotiate Without Negativity – Matthew 5:25 Luke 4? John 15:13

Servant leaders practice leadership that involves settling matters without becoming negative about the matter or individuals involved in the negotiation. The art of discussion and collaboration that leads to agreement without attacking one's character and reputation and influencing others by speaking uncivilly about them to others is in desperate need of resurrection.

Jesus taught His disciples to settle disagreements with their adversaries to avoid being taken before the judge and officials because they run the risk of being thrown into prison. Servant leaders should guard their reputations and cover the reputations of others by resisting to devalue them with their negative words.

"The first time you say something, it's heard. The second time, it's recognized, and the third time it's learned." ~John Maxwell

T is Teaching Without Tyranny – Luke 9:43-62

The art of teaching involves causing followers to acquire knowledge or skill in some area. Teaching also involves showing or explaining how to do something. There are many ways that leaders teach. However, one should never be with absolute oppressive power and authority.

Servant leaders are not dictators. They are not ruthless, cruel, or unreasonable. Their leadership is not a reign of terror, bullying, and desire of absolute power and authority in the lives of their followers. A servant leader recognizes the headship and lordship of God as supreme leader in the lives of believers. Jesus modeled the art of taking advantage of every teachable moment and utilized the art of storytelling through the use of parables. He was with them, He allowed them to be *with* Him in ministry, in disputes, in rebukes, performing miracles, solitude, praying, and suffering. He was honest, open, and transparent, even though they did not always comprehend the meaning of His words and works.

"People do not care how much you know until they know how much you care." ~John Maxwell

Are you wondering…should we assume that servant leaders also expect their followers to be Christ-followers? The resurrection of servant leadership empowers followers to evaluate and compare the policies, procedures, philosophies, and principles with the leadership modeled by Jesus. The use of biblical checks and balances can be preventative measures for the misuse of power and authority. Jesus was in authority and under authority, yet He submitted Himself to the leadership of the Father in all things. Likewise, the resurrection of servant leadership requires that leaders should lead themselves and be in subjection to Jesus in all things. Leaders who dismiss themselves from Jesus' authority are in danger of opening the door to pride and ungodly behaviors. The Apostle Paul suggests the perfect attitude of a servant leader by empowering his followers to only follow him as he follows Christ (1 Corinthians 11:1). Servant leaders living in harmony with this principle profess their lives an open book and subject to analysis by their followers. When a leader derails himself from the path of following Jesus, they automatically relinquish their authority and right to be heard and followed as a leader. The Spirit of God does not submit Himself to an ungodly spirit in leadership or otherwise.

In order to be an effective servant leader, one must consider the mandate to abide in Jesus and serve according to His new covenant to love one another and in so doing the world will know they are His disciples (John 15:4-5; John 13:34-35). The ancient fruit of the Spirit, love, and the biblical principle of *abiding* in Jesus are often the missing components that ensure leaders not only begin well but finish well and leave a legacy that continues to turn the world upside down because followers are impacted and empowered to continue the legacy began by the supreme servant leader, Jesus the Christ. The true value of a leader is the ability to reproduce disciples that look more like Jesus than themselves. This resurrection legacy becomes the purpose, plan, and predetermined will of God throughout His world and reproduces organically.

Servant Leadership Resurrection Application Questions

1. *What do you believe is your current leadership style?*
2. *Who was or currently is your leadership mentor?*
3. *In what ways are you leading like your leadership mentor? Like Jesus?*
4. *What can you begin to do to resurrect your leadership to look more like Jesus?*
5. *What are some things you need to remove from your leadership style that do not resemble Jesus?*

"I am an Imprint Leader"

Dr. Sofia Lu Abdiwahid

Dr. Lul Abdiwahid is the founder and CEO of Pure Pearl Foundation. The foundation was founded in 2016 and has its main office in Mombasa city. Pure Pearl's main objective is to transform the lives of vulnerable women, youth and children in Africa through relief and sustainable economic development projects. Dr. Lul's inspiration to establish a charitable organization was triggered by the conflict that exists between the cultural beliefs and prosperity of women and youths in the local communities. She witnessed first-hand the effects of harmful practices on victims of female genital mutilation, gender based violence, child marriages and the general women's struggle for basic human rights.

This experience drove her to think of effective ways to solve this problem. A law degree from the UK was a great starting point; she joined the Kenya School of Law and got admitted to the Bar. After which, she set up Abdiwahid and Associates law firm. Through her practice, she handled over 100 pro bono cases on gender inequality, discrimination and gender based violence. She is also the founder of one of the most competitive professional cleaning and waste management companies in Kenya, Salu Solutions Ltd. The company specializes in professional cleaning services for industrial, commercial and domestic needs having served over 150 prestigious businesses. Since its inception, the company has created employment for over 110 youths and women who traditionally couldn't be employed due to their lack of requisite experience and qualifications.

Dr. Lul is passionate about women and youth empowerment. She hopes that a time will come when equal opportunities will be available to everyone no matter their gender. Moreover, economic and social justice is her dream for every woman, youth and child in Africa. Through the foundation, Dr. Lul's vision to have an educated and skillful population in the near future is being fulfilled gradually. She believes that a peaceful living community will be attained by empowering the masses and that is her major focus.

Dr. Lul Abdiwahid holds credible credentials. She holds an Honoree Doctorate in Humanities from United Graduate College and Seminary International, USA, a Masters in International Law (LLM) from the University of Warwick England and LLB from University of Kent, Canterbury. She has been awarded the World Civility Ambassador, Ambassador for Peace from the Universal Federation of Peace and has also been named among the top 100 most influential Kenyan Muslim. She was named the World Civility Icon woman of the year, Africa 2019.

Civility Imprint

Dr. Lul Abdiwahid was also awarded for Leading Light of Greatness, University of Greatness London, UK and became the Goodwill Ambassador through Humanity Equity Value, Trinidad and Tobago.

Additionally, Dr. Lul is a member of the Law Society of Kenya (LSK), Mombasa Law Society (MLS), Federation of Women Lawyers in Kenya (FIDA), Chartered Institute of Arbitrators (CIARB Kenya), IChange Nations and also a member of the Standards Tribunal.

Dr. Lul Abdiwahid is an entrepreneur, an Advocate of the High Court of Kenya and a philanthropist who enjoys reading motivational books and traveling.

"I am an Imprint Leader"

By: Dr. Sofia Lu Abdiwahid

Challenging life impacts that triggered me to rise to leadership and lead courageously, leaving my Life Civility Imprints that will live on for eternity:

I come from a society that enforces endogenous cultural norms and barriers on women. Women are denied social, political and leadership privileges. Girls are seen as possessions and they are married off at a young age. They are depicted as weak and vulnerable; they get discriminated against and oppressed. Our women are voiceless. They have a limited privilege to education access, employment opportunities, and leadership positions.

Being in the field, I have dealt with many issues affecting women first-hand. Issues like gender-based violence, female genital mutilation (FGM), teenage girls and women dealing with unsafe abortions and unwanted pregnancies, youth unemployment, growing illiteracy levels, and limited access to education or training to equip one with skills.

Also, growing up in a different cultural setting where I experienced inclusivity of women in the society inspired confidence in me and dreams I had. The experiences empowered me to break cultural norms and barriers existing in our society to become a civility ambassador.

Share how leaders can learn and lead based on your IMPRINT:

Leaders can learn and lead based on my Imprint by recognizing the value of educating and empowering women and children in society. They could utilize programs that inform, enlighten, and encourage young girls and boys in the society. Such programs will encourage, inspire, and inform the young girls and women that they can grow into strong, capable women and live their life purpose.

I would urge leaders to encourage the youth to know who they are and develop themselves... provide them with tools, financial support, and mentorship programs that will equip them with the necessary life-skills. Also, leaders could take the initiative to recognize and award personalities that have been instrumental in advocating for women's equality and rights.

Who or what has been your motivation to stay focused on your Civility Imprint as a leadership?

My mentees who are women, young girls and boys are my motivation. Also my biggest motivation has been my mother and grandmother. Even though they didn't receive the formal education I got, they encouraged me to break the cultural norms and barriers. Also, being connected with God has been my motivation... I believe by focusing on God everything is possible. I can be all that I want to be if I work hard. There's absolutely no limit to what I can do.

Also, growing up in England where I saw inclusivity of women really motivated me to keep working on my dream. I have found motivation by interacting with great women leaders, plus facing criticism when growing up inspired me to remain persistent on my goals.

What is your favorite quote and why?

"What good is freedom of speech if women don't have a voice?".

We all have a purpose. Every soul on earth is born with a unique gift. And life is truly about finding, developing, and utilizing your God-given gift. In God's eyes, we're equal. But a patriarchal society enforces gender imbalance, rendering women to be voiceless and less important. Women are told to be submissive and not to speak up. They face discrimination, oppression, and they are denied education and leadership opportunities. In a society that encourages freedom of speech, it's of no good if women don't have a voice... when they can't develop themselves to live their life purpose.

What organization are you with? How are you practicing Civility in Your organization?

I work with Pure Pearl Foundation, an international charitable organization whose main objective is to transform the lives of vulnerable women and children in Africa. I'm practicing civility by giving young girls and women education opportunities and mentorship programs that empower them to develop themselves and live their life purpose. We empower women, plus young girls and boys to have a voice and learn leadership skills. We provide women and the youth with work and education opportunities. Our organization helps orphaned kids through education and work opportunities. We work with young girls to mentor them into responsible adults, including providing school girls with sanitary towels.

"I am an Imprint Leader"

Angela Gaines

Angela Gaines is founder of Imani Images, which is an empowerment series and workshop/ministry that she does to lift women up in their everyday lives. She states that image means "I'm awesome God's girl everyday".

She lives in Greenville, South Carolina and received her Bachelor of Science degree in Psychology from Lander University. She is now in the process of pursuing a certification in life coaching that specializes in women's issues & ministries. She is a licensed social worker and licensed certified addictions counselor II from the state of South Carolina. She is a certified image consultant/coach and presently in management with Mary Kay cosmetics. Angela earned her 1st free MK car in 2017!! She is also a Traci Lynn jewelry stylist. What is most important to

Angela is her role of being an evangelist and motivational speaker for God. She loves her gift of empowering others to love and know the power of the Lord.

Angela has been working with women and families for over 29 years. She has assisted others in loving themselves spiritually, physically, and mentally. She is widely respected for her broad range of workshops on image and empowerment. She has worked with many businesses, organization and churches. She teaches others the steps to a new beginning.

She has served on many community boards in the area. Currently, she is the chairperson for Minority Diversity Council for The Blood Connection. She has assisted and served on a witness prevention committee for breast cancer awareness. Ms. Gaines has also served on Pink Ghost Health and Breast Cancer program and is a graduate of Phyillis Wheatley Leadership Greenville Program. She is coordinator & creator of the women's group at Bethlehem Baptist church called " B.A.S.E" (Building All Sisters Everyday), praise team worship leader and Sunday school teacher for teens class. Last but not least she is a leader in greeter's ministry.

Angela has been married for 32 years to her high school sweetheart and they have one son and one granddaughter living in the NC area.

Angela is on a mission to help others in pursuing a positive image, attitude and a love for god. She feels this is necessary for achievement and success!!!

her motto is:

"With God's love and guidance many doors are opened." Her message is to keep evangelizing this message because purpose for her is to empower others to find beauty inside and out.

My Journey Out of The dark Cave
By Angela Gaines

I married at a young age to my high-school sweetheart. My parents didn't want me to do this. We were young and we had dated all through school. We were best friends and feeding off of each other, even though our backgrounds were different. His family parties all the time and I was isolated. My mother didn't want us to be out of her sight and was very strict. We still made it work and went through growing together, struggling together and praying together. My journey always has been to be driven, work for me and be my own boss. I went to school and graduated from college with a degree in psychology. I work with families and children with abuse and addiction issues. This kind of work was emotional altogether and you have to let it go. I became a mother after a few years of marriage and love raising my son. I never thought my relationship or marriage would change and it did. We always feel we have the perfect marriage and family, but that is never true. Addictions, disloyalty and lies became an issue in my home, so it fell apart. I never thought this would affect my own life and it was hidden from me for a while. I was broken and the person I loved left me that first time during the holiday season. My son and I celebrated alone and was shocked with what hit us, but that is how drugs affect a family. It can tear a family apart. This person was no longer my husband, the best friend or child's father I knew. I did not want my son to suffer and I knew what addiction and pain did to families because I was helping people with the same issues. Money was gone, bills were due and then there was the agony of not letting my family know about what happened. It was a struggle and I didn't want them to know and feel sorry for me or to say I told you so. We separated the first time so I could heal and so he could as well. I moved on being the strong determined woman that I was supposed to be. I moved back home with my parents and tried to refocus. Eventually, we became a family again after my husband did some healing and recovery. Trust was huge for me and I became a beast and did not want to be a submissive wife like the Bible wanted me to be. I needed to have control and I was not going to let this mess happen again.

There were relapses and some conflicts, but we still overcame and became more involved in church and healed some of the hurt. But there were times when drama happened because of his addiction and he got into trouble. A job was hard for him and anger was there in our home. This anger laid in my heart and I was tired of being the one who was trying to keep our home together. We did grow at times for the sake of our son, and we wanted him to know the best and be the best. I wanted to protect him because he was not going to be a drug addict or a nobody. We kept him involved in activities in the community and in sports and in great schools. Today he is a fine young man because we both wanted that for him and we wanted both of us to raise him. But the hurt and emotional issues and some feelings of blame and feelings of being lost lead to us growing apart and after 22 years of marriage we decided to go our separate ways. We still to this day love each other and know that we will be connected because of our growing up together and because of us sharing a son.

I am a passionate woman and love God! He has given me the gift to empower and encourage and lift a woman or man up. But especially women! I am a businesswoman with a company that makes a woman beautiful and the philosophy of God, family and career.

I love speaking to others and letting them know the passion you must have in life and to know God first. I have grown to know me and speak of my journey. Even if you lose material things or a person you love, you can still overcome and move on. I am a mover and a Shaker and there were times my husband, family, and others will say it would never work or you can't do it, but I would keep pushing and it has made me be successful to this day. Remain respectful and do you. Don't lose sight of who you are, even if life gives you a curveball. Go a different direction. People are jealous of you and will hurt you. Yes, and say you are nothing, but God says you are. I am still growing and God is not through with me yet! I am moving ahead with advancing more, building a successful empire, leaving a legacy, rebuilding my marriage and my life coaching career. But mostly, spiritually remaining on a new journey of loving and learning about Me! I am and do have my power to make dreams happen and be there for my son and family always. This book is for the woman who are ready to change and make love continue to happen even during crisis.

Loving and Owning yourself!!

Learning to love who you are and your
abilities is a day-to-day journey. It is one of
exploring your actions, motives, feelings and
thoughts. On this journey called life, we must
remember everybody will not love you, talk to
you, like what you do, or want you to be a
part of the team. But you must learn to keep it
moving. I call it (K.I.M). Loving oneself
comes with taking a personal inventory of
your gifts, talents and born given actions. Ask
yourself, do I like me? If you don't like
yourself, how can you expect others to like
you or love you. How many of you can
remember a time when you weren't picked to
be on a team or they did not choose you for
that job or position. Hey, we all have been
there when we weren't chosen to be the mate
in a relationship. We were disappointed, hurt
and sometimes broken. But there are key
things to put in place to begin to love oneself.
These three P's are very significant and
valuable. Change is a journey and you cannot
move forward in life without loving who You
Are. It is a peel back process. Furthermore, it
begins with Purpose, Passion and Power.
Purpose equals having self-confidence and
knowing your why. It begins with changing
the mindset, the desire and pattern of who

you are. It's a feeling or an 'It" that never, never goes away. It is a spiritual connection that stays involved with you, even when you try to run away or detour, it shows back up. This is your time to do a self-inventory. Passion is described in Webster dictionary as a burning desire to have it. This is an attitude that is so deep and strong that no one can stand in your way. You would do whatever it takes to make it happen and you will find yourself loving the person inside. You feel like a winner who can stand alone. You will affirm the beautiful person inside every day. Power is a huge action and feeling of oneself. When you affirm and love you more, you will rise up with an ultimate victory in your mind. You no longer think in the can't category. You walk and communicate like a winner. There is a shift of belief and connection that makes you move unapologetically. So wake up each day and affirm. I am great and great things happen to me. I am powerful and powerful things happen to me! I am beautiful, I love Me! Just create the best You ever! Celebrate oneself Victoriously! Angela Gaines, LBSW, LCACII Life/Parenting Coach, Motivational Speaker, Community Advocate & Businesswoman

"As an Imprint Leader"

By: Angela Gaines

One of the impacts that have helped me to want to lead others is the challenges that women face every single day. After 29 years of working with women and children, I've seen the suffering that they go through with poverty , addiction and lack of self-esteem. This has led me to my gift of empowering women's lives and to help them to see how important they are when you put God first, yourself second than others last. When I think of the aspect of "Lead" in my mind, L means to Lift someone up and guide them to a new level, E means helping others to be enthusiastic about life and face the challenge and A equals your attitude needs to change and remain positive daily. D equals the determination to make great things happen and trust and believe it. I have been that broken woman who felt alone who believed that life was over after going through relationship issues and addictions with a mate. It was not easy but with spiritual belief and self-determination it helped me to move on to know that life is amazing and awesome. Lead by example and with integrity and be transparent about what you been through. Those lessons strengthens another person. Organizations that I'm currently a part of Nurturing Parenting and Families program, graduate of the Phyllis Wheatley leadership development program in Greenville, Past Chairwoman of the the Blood Connection diversity board. I am also a member of National Association of Alcohol and Drug Council. Angela is a Licensed Certified Addiction Counselor II for state of SC. Also currently an entrepreneur, life/ parenting coach and Sales Director with Mary Kay Cosmetics. Angela feels with each role the focus of empowering women and others of enriching their lives with beauty inside and out. My focus is for every person to see how special they are and to use what gifts that God has given them to impact the world in every way.

Civility Imprint

"I am an Imprint Leader"

By:

Dr Eric Holmes

As we journey through life we will have challenges and trials but we must overcome with triumph and victory. Impacts that cause me to lead courageous is standing on the shoulders of others that have gone before me and left impact and footprints. Leaders can learn from me as I have learned from others but also what God placed in me to triumph and endure and never quit but show up every day. My mother who transitioned was a great influence and motivation. Now my older sister, my Bishop and First Lady keep me motivated by watching them evolve and many others I surround myself with of positive influence. As I speak many places, I'm motivated by sharing my story yet being reminded the work Christ done for me. I am challenged to do more, to rise and Make An Impact. I am with John's Hopkins, Bethel Temple and my brand, The Power of the Seed.

We should leave a legacy plus a bona-fide IMPRINT for others to follow but show up and make Impact that will leave an impression to change lives, communities and the world . Let's work to make and be the CHANGE.

"I am an Imprint Leader"

Latrice Scott

Latrice Scott is a Sr. Manager of Talent Acquisition, with over 15 years of experience, coaching and developing teams in the formation of successful acquisition strategies and organizational change. She is not ashamed of the gospel and also has served as a licensed Evangelist in the Church of God in Christ for over 25 years, supporting wife to Pastor Allen L. Scott and has held multiple roles serving in the house of God as Minister of Music and Women's Ministry Leader. As an avid learner, she also has achieved a Bachelor's and Master's in Human Resource Management and is currently a PHD candidate at Capella University.

Civility Imprint

Born to parents Pastor Eric D. and Delois Brooks, Latrice was dedicated as a child back to God for use in His service and the glory of His Kingdom. From the time of her youth, it is irrefutable that God's hand and favor have guided her every move. There has never been a question that her life was purposed for Greatness. She has always been passionate for the things of God and most recently has been zealous about sharing God's love with women of all ages to inspire, encourage and motivate them to love themselves no matter what they have gone through.

Latrice is a woman of prayer and faith, which was demonstrated when she prayed her husband back to life in 2006 after a fatal heart attack rendered the need for a heart transplant. Her favorite past time is traveling and sharing her testimony of healing, faith and prayer. Latrice has 7 children and 21 grandchildren. In her free time, she enjoys spending time with her husband, children and grandchildren who affectionately call her GiGi.

It's Necessary
By: Latrice Scott

From the time we are born, we are faced with our first issue when we enter this world. The ability to breathe our first breath of life. As a result, we are assaulted by the physician who hits you on the back so that our first breath is taken thus activating the functioning of the lungs. The hit was necessary in order for the baby to survive outside of the womb. If the hit had not been given, the lungs wouldn't have been activated to work properly.

I don't know about you, but I am not a fan of getting hit. Physical hits can hurt, sting and leave you with a bruise. Mental hits affect your mind and leave you disoriented, confused and depressed. Hits to the soul can be some of the most painful and have long lasting effects. Regardless, taking any type of hit does not feel good. However examining the lesson from the life of a newborn baby, the hit, no matter how devastating is necessary.

A hit that was administered to me, was when my husband died in my driveway. The blow was devastating in so many ways. To God be the glory through much faith and prayer he was brought back to life and lived long enough to receive a heart transplant 4 months later. While forever grateful to God for giving him back to me, I didn't know back then how this hit would impact my life as an instant caregiver. This hit was a blow to my mind, body and soul for over 14 years.

For 14 years, I have been a caregiver to my husband, work full time as a Sr. Manager of Talent Acquisition, an Evangelist in the Church of God in Christ and raised 7 kids of which all but 2 graduated college. On top of all this, I was working on a Master's degree. I was burning the candle at both ends. My hit gave me life. However, I was living for others and putting myself last. I ran on empty for years, pouring out into my husband, family, work, church and any others requiring my time.

In my mind, I was fine. I was oblivious of how close I was to self-destruction. Smiling on the outside, masking the pain. Only my Father, God really knew what was going on inside. I was literally committing suicide in my mind, body and soul and was suffering from being too busy pleasing others to know that I needed to breathe and put on my oxygen mask.

From 2015-2019, I literally felt like a punching bag taking hit after hit. During this time, my husband's kidneys failed causing him to go on dialysis 3 days a week. Every 3-6 months he was in the hospital for extended stays. Each year for 4 years, he would go into the hospital around the end of December and stay for 6 months. During these stays, each year he would be on life support with a thin line between life and death. Each time his transplanted heart and kidney disease worsened ultimately rending him in end stage renal failure.

In May 2019, everything came to a screeching halt for me. My husband was being released from an extended stay in the hospital when the doctors came into the room and told us he had stage 4 renal cancer. I immediately felt numb all over not knowing if I could take it anymore. The next few days turned out to be some of the darkest days in my life. I was literally exhausted in my mind, body and soul. I felt like this was the final blow that would knock me out for good.

I tried to work and my manager forced me to take leave due to everything I had going on. I couldn't focus on anything and found my health was failing with my diabetes and blood pressure severely uncontrolled. During my time off, I finally went to the doctor and left with 2 different types of insulin that I had to take 4 times a day in addition to more meds given to control both the diabetes and blood pressure.

As I sat in my office crying, looking at all of that medicine and insulin I had to take, I prayed to God to send me something or someone to help me through this. I felt defeated because I even went to see a therapist who diagnosed me with extreme depression and anxiety. All the while the devil was beating me up whispering in my ear, "Now what are you going to do, Mighty Woman of God?" Even though I was in my worst state, I felt like Job and I raised my voice to let the devil know in no uncertain terms that I would live and not die and declare the works of the Lord!

A couple of days later, a good friend of mine called me and introduced me to some supplements that she said may help with my diabetes. Little did I know something so simple and natural would change my life. I started the supplements and much to my surprise they lowered my blood sugar and helped me to eat better. I began walking and the weight started to slowly come off, I was able to come off the insulin and blood pressure medicine. All of my blood work began to stabilize and I started to feel like normal.

During this time, I realized it was not until I started to care for myself that I began to feel better in my mind body and soul. Self-care became my priority and my medicine. It reminded me of how I was on the road to self-destruction because I didn't care enough about my own wellbeing. As things began to improve, I wanted to share with everyone the supplements and mindset shift that occurred. By sharing my story, I was able to help many people change their lives just as mine changed.

In the beginning of my story I shared how taking a hit is necessary. Had I not taken such a violent blow, I would have never been able to see how bad off I was. Denial is real and deadly. As long as one is in denial, they will continue to wander along the same path of destruction. Through my experience I am able to bring others out of the pit.

I know two mentees who were at their wits end with their health when they came to me. I shared with them how I too was right there and through the help of God and the supplements, I feel and look 100% better. One of them came to me crying and ready to commit suicide because of how the weight had her bound in so many aspects of her life. With the help of God and sharing with her that regardless what the enemy told her that, she was more than a conqueror through Jesus that loves her. Twelve months later, this same person has a new outlook on life. She lost 90 pounds in a year and has done a total lifestyle change. It didn't happen overnight. However, through prayer, sacrifice and steadfastness, she maximized self-care techniques to tap into self-healing.

My imprint is simple, I love me! I can't help anyone else if I am not well. Complete wholeness in the mind, body and soul is a priority to my well-being. Sharing the message of self-care and its importance has saved my life and many others that I have been blessed to coach. The core part of the self-care process is to know your worth.

- Know your **w**orth
    - o Know who you are and your value
- You are an **o**vercomer
    - o Know that you are more than a conqueror.
  - He **r**estores my soul.
      - o Get some rest – stop running on empty
- **T**ake care of your temple.
    - o Stay fit for duty by taking care of mind, body and soul
- Celebrate your **h**aters.
    - o Haters are necessary to bring you into your full potential.

All of the hits that have come my way were necessary! They have conditioned me and made me strong. I may have gotten knocked down, but in my weakness, God was strong in my life and He helped me to get back up again. If you are reading this and resonating with my experience, I would love to help you too through any tough situations you may be experiencing. Know the hits come to make you strong and sometimes you need a life jacket to help you navigate through the waters.

Remember, it's necessary to bring you to your destiny. It's necessary so that you can breathe the breath of life. Whatever it you may be facing is only going to make you stronger, wiser and better.

"I am an Imprint Leader"

Dr. Sabeeta Bidasie-Singh

Sabeeta Bidasie-Singh is the CEO of Cardinal Services LLC, Partner in Blockchain for Education Training (BEST) and a University Professor in Houston. Sabeeta' s Doctorate in Business Administration tackles the issue of Agility and Transformation during Disruption head-on. Sabeeta consults for clients in the space of Strategy and Realignment, Diversity and Empowerment, Agile Transformation and Customer Experience. She also works on the back end of the concepts she implements for her clients through Instructional Design for Higher Education in Policy and Strategy Formulation, Business Decision Modelling, Entrepreneurship and Organizational Behavior. Sabeeta brings over 25 years of international work experience across a number of sectors in Australia, Asia, North America, Costa Rica, Cuba and The Caribbean. As a Partner in Health Blockchain Security Services (HCISS), she looks after the international growth strategy for the business - HCISS is a technology company that offers Future Security for the health of Blockchain Networks. Sabeeta is a STEM champion and has worked with IBM in making education affordable and accessible to rural communities by building Regional Learning Centers and the IBM Center of Innovation to address the industry skills shortages by offering IBM professional certifications within the undergrad programs. Over the period 2016 – 2019 the program upskilled over 5,000 graduates and enrolled over 10, 000 students in the Regional Learning Centers in Malaysia. She has designed Diversity and Empowerment programs for Industry and Higher Educational Institutes in Australia, Malaysia, the United States of America and the United Kingdom with a commitment to equity and sustained leadership. These programs are deployed across private and public institutions and organizations and tied into employability objectives. Sabeeta has consulted on the institutional aspect of Educational Reform in terms of: (1) Student Motivation and Engagement (2) Learning designed with Employability Outcomes (3) Education for Lifelong Learning (4) Effective use of Resources (5) Intelligence Accountability (6) High Quality Teaching and Leadership (7) Alignment and Coherence and reducing the Achievement Gaps. Sabeeta implemented the No Child Left Behind program at North American University and reduced the gaps between Minority and Majority students across the Independent School District in Houston. She has transformed educational programs in Australia and Malaysia to ensure that activated learning replaces Rote learning in the Instruction Design and delivery. The shift included more conceptual learning concepts embedded in teaching and learning practices which helped over 10,000 students build stronger retention and applied learning skills. Sabeeta is an advisory board member in areas of Diversity, Empowerment and Educational Reform in South Africa, Nigeria, Adelaide, Queensland, Kuala Lumpur, Trinidad and the United States of America. She writes for several Diversity and Empowerment publications and her work is widely published. Sabeeta was a facilitator on the Lead India Conference very recently but has also been a guest speaker and Conference Lead at several conferences across the United States of America. She implemented the Industry Advisory Board at Inti International University in Kuala Lumpur, Malaysia that engaged industry partners to align with the learning outcomes delivered in the various Undergraduate streams and encouraged involvement in identifying gaps between program delivery and market skills demanded for various streams. This greatly improved the University's visibility among employers throughout Malaysia and assisted with graduate employability statistics.

Life Can Be Beautiful Even Through A Crisis

By Dr. Sabeeta Bidasie-Singh

Hello, readers! I am Dr. Sabeeta Bidasei Singh, and I'm the CEO of Cardinal Services, LLC, based out of Houston. I am a global consultant and I work in different parts of the world, primarily Asia, here in the U.S., and the Caribbean. I have spent the last 25 years gathering best practices across a number of fields. My doctorate is on agility and transformation during times of disruption.

In the last year and a half, I've really had to put every bit of research from my doctorate to work, as we were trying to transform and pivot during these very disruptive and uncertain times. These times were brought to us through no choice of ours, but by something we never even saw coming. The global pandemic was a weapon in the dark and it totally disrupted our lives. We all had to pivot. We had to transform from a business perspective, from a professional perspective, from a personal perspective. Every element of my research has been put into play at working with clients, and even on a personal level to scale up during these times. That's a little bit about me on a professional level.

On a personal level, I am a mother of two wonderful boys. I've got an eighteen year old who just graduated from high school. He's headed off to Texas ENM very soon. My older son is twenty one. He is at the University of Houston doing a degree in music production, but he's also an up and coming avid rapper or hip hop artist. He is such an amazing child. He writes his music and he produces. He's so passionate about it, and for me, I support him 100% and I have had a lot of pushback.

People challenge me when they say, "You've been an educator for the last 15 years, but your son is into music." I answer, "Well, you know what, fuel your passion, and

I would not be a good mother if I didn't support my child's dream."

So, that's me where I am and what I'm doing right now. I support a number of charities. I am the Director of Training and Development for the Lead India Global Foundation and we are mission-based. We are across many continents and touching lives every day.

Right now we are very engaged with what's going on the ground in India. It's no surprise at the number of deaths. Those numbers are reported all over the media. It's very sad and it is alarming, but it has also shaken us when we look at our human factor. We are getting tele-doctors brought up every week. We have a weekly session where we bring on medical professionals. We bring on nutritionists.

This morning, we had some grief counselor's talk to people about dealing with loss, the struggles of what's going on, how to face pain, how to process pain and how to prepare yourself for a loss. We are doing these amazing things as an organization, and we are trying to reach as many people as possible.

I truly believe that a positive attitude can have a positive influence on your life. People sometimes can't believe that I am old enough to have adult children. Staying young has always been something at heart. So, I go to my kid's soccer game. I get out in the backyard and I kick the ball with them. My boys may struggle sometimes, but it's just the wanting to be a part of everything they're doing, and sharing these moments with them. For me, that is so important.

My son just received an award for soccer on his varsity team, and I was about to put it on social media. I said, "You know what? I want to put the right phrase and coin it nicely." But I was going to say something like, "When everything you want is right in front of you..."

That is important because, far too often, I see people reaching and reaching for so much that they're not certain about. Yet, if they just stop and look around, do a quick scan of their environment, there's so much that is right in front of them that they're not even seeing.

If they were to look back in reflection five years from now, they would think, "How did I miss that moment?" Do not miss the things that are in front of you! That is so important. While you're thinking long term, always have that bit of myopia so you see the important stuff in front of you. Time is not constant, it moves. We have to be dynamic and move with it, but it's important to enjoy the moment.

Earlier this week, I was talking to an audience in India and we were addressing COVID-19, the second wave. I want to bring this into perspective. We are looking at alarming statistics, the number of deaths. But are we looking at a recovery? Are we looking at how much our life is changing? Are we looking at all the humanitarian efforts on the ground?

I am seeing more humanity in people now than I saw two years ago. I think people are more connected with the value of meaning and the essence of brotherhood. So while COVID may have thrown a curve ball at us, I think humanity is coming back into play. We were losing touch of that and it's really important when we talk about this change. We get wrapped up in the race of life and we miss moments. COVID made us stop. COVID made us stop and say, "Hang on, let's stop, press that pause button before we can hit reset."

Like any tragedy, there are lives that are being lost, but we are also reaching out. I've never seen a bigger outreach than what we are experiencing now with this wave of humanity. That's our pause button. That's our moment where we stop and we look at how our children are growing, how we ourselves have changed. We're going to stop and say: "This is our present frame. We get a chance to change the future. Let's do it. Let's do it now."

The broadcast program I mentioned was done in India. I want you to know that India has recorded one of the fastest growing economies in the last five years. English is naturally spoken and is a readily acceptable language. I'm fourth generation Indian. I am also a Caribbean girl. I was born on a tiny island of one million people, called Trinidad and Tobago. I am the great, great granddaughter of an indentured servant.

My forefathers were brought into the Caribbean when slavery was abolished. The first set of voyages was primarily dominated by men, and it became a primary role of the females in preserving family values, preserving culture and traditions. I think it's really important because what I saw in the Caribbean, over time we lost our natural language.

My great-grandfather would have been speaking one of the Hindi or Indian dialects, but in the Caribbean it was not passed on to us. Our food transformed, our lifestyle is very different. So when I go to India, I go as a visitor, which I am because I am more Caribbean based on my roots. People naturally walk up to me and start speaking Hindi. Then, I open my mouth, and they're like, "Oh.", because my accent is very Caribbean. Then, I try to explain, "Look, I want to learn. There's this gap."

That is my way of trying to reach back to things that are important and fundamental to whom I am today, because had my great-grandfather not gotten onto that ship and gotten to Trinidad, I would not have been the diverse personality I am.

I have had the privilege of living and working in countries like Australia, Asia, throughout the U.S., I've been through all the entire Caribbean and worked in the Caribbean, every island. So for me, that diversity is so important. But to enjoy that diversity, I have to know who I was and where I come from. That whole movement has been working on creating me and leading me to the place where I am now. That is so important to me personally, knowing my roots.

One of the things I think we should talk about is stereotypes. We live in a society that tells us who we should be based on how we look. Society dictates how we should behave, how we should dress. We have been conforming to those rules of society. Far too often, those stereotypical perspectives of who we are and who we should be based on our physical looks, dictate the rest of our lives.

I have a friend and prior to having children she was a perfect figure 8, so to speak, in terms of having an absolutely gorgeous body and everything. Our bodies go through a lot through childhood and that whole childbearing process and it is beautiful. Now, five years later, she's battling the bulge, and I have seen her confidence erode. She used to be so sure of herself and so positive, and because of the labeling that society places on you if we add on a few chunks of pounds anywhere, or things that are not conforming to who we should be, people use remarks like, "Oh my God, you used to look so..." And I would stop them like, "Used to what? This is me. This is who I am now. Appreciate the "me" I am now."

I don't give those words any space in my

head and I tell my friend the same thing, "You are not who you were prior to childhood. You are such a more mature individual. You have processed so much. You've given birth. You've given a gift to the world. You have brought life in."

I would not even go back to who I was prior to my kids. I tell her the same thing, "I am so much more as a mother than I was as a person before bringing lives into this world."

We all contribute to the world, whether you're a mother, a father, whether you adopt a child. We're giving back. But don't let society tell you who you should be, how you should look based on these perfect images. There is no perfect. We are not living in a perfect world.

Another passion of mine is professional development training and working with Dr. Kalam's Foundation in India. It supports key sustainable development goals. Things like poverty reduction and access to education, access to good health care. Those are the sustainable goals that are very important to

me. Anything I support, any venture I
support, has to align with my vision.

I believe that the alleviation of poverty is
so important, especially if you've been to
India, you know there are so many contrasts.
You've got some very wealthy, but you've got
some extremely impoverished as well. How
do we create a bit more equity in society?
How do we move past those lines that
segregate society? Poverty alleviation is one of
them and, one of the ways we can alleviate
poverty is through education.

People often ask what motivates me. Well
let me tell you. I was born on an island of one
million people. That is not a very big place!
Where I live in Houston, my city is way bigger
than the country or the island I was born in
and I have worked in the largest continent in
the world.

For me, the ability to be this island girl
and represent my country, gives me that inner
fire and motivation. I've never stepped away
from who I am. My accent over the last 20
years has never changed because that is my

identity. What you see with me is what you get, and I'm not going to conform to those models that society expects. I speak my tone, I speak the language. You want to listen to me, you tune in. If I'm not appealing to you, that's fine. There's somebody else that will reach you because there are more of me around.

However, aligning to the lead in the foundation was very important to me because I have been extremely fortunate in my life. If you study Maslow's Hierarchy of Needs, I am at that point of self-actualization, where I want to achieve all those things I've set out for myself.

I am going to be forty years old in a couple of months, and for me, I think it's time to start giving back. My kids are in a great place. I feel as though I have things that I can share with the world, and my gifts, my journeys, my travels, my experiences, even if I can touch one life one day at a time, that's very meaningful for me and that's why I do what I do.

I'm big on diversity. I'm a big DE&I, Diversity, Equality, and Inclusion champion. If you look at my resume, if you look at all the work I do, I work with a lot of women. I work in impoverished communities and I do a lot of outreach.

Far too often, and I say this with no malice, I see women who have climbed the corporate ladder, and they're sitting in what I call the queen bee syndrome, where they've gotten to this top spot, and rather than make a way for other women, they're actually stifling other women and stunting their growth.

That could be due to a number of factors. It could be the fact that the places that are open are limited, and these women at the top want to hog it, or they're just not sure about themselves, or they don't trust other women. I don't know what it is, but if we are going to promote women and open that door for the women who are going to come behind us, we've got to hold it open. We can't be halfway there and speak the language like, "Hey, I'm a champion of change. Hey, I want more women out there. I want to see more women climbing that ladder."

We're speaking the language, but how many of us are walking the walk? Far too often, when I work with clients or when I look at corporate structures, I see a lot of hot air. I see very few activity-based leaders, female leaders, actually hand-holding others and taking them on the journey. That is what we need.

To bring things full circle for this chapter, I was asked to share my thoughts on resurrection. My definition of resurrection is Nirvana. It's life after death. When you've hit that lowest point and you feel you can't go on, you dig deep, and you find that wind, you find that little gust of energy, just that little gleam of the light, and you hold onto hope. That is your way out; that little glimmer of light.

Have you been in a tunnel where it's so dark, and it's just a crevice of light? Hold on to that light. Don't focus on the darkness, stick to the light. Keep your eye on that path, and you will rise because sometimes we have to lose it all before we can begin. It's okay, it's perfectly okay, to lose it all and start over, because when you're starting over, you're starting from a point of experience, and that is amazing. That's going to chart your journey.

As the wheel races on, just stay grounded. Stay grounded to ensure who you are. If you're true to whom you are, your identity will be carved out of it.

You don't have to be an everyone, you just need to be who you are, and be that someone.

"I am an Imprint Leader"

Leila Awale

Her courage and determination to conquer from within has inspired their own untapped talents and infinite potential.

Leila has done several talks and programs that have transformed the lives of countless men and woman across the country. We talk about nutrition for our health, we talk about exercise for our health. In this day and age, the biggest issue we are facing with our health is our mental health. I want to help people wire or rewire their brains so that they can prosper and live the best life they can, no matter the situation.

Leila's programs are centered around corporates, groups, organizations, community, entrepreneurs, women and leaders.

Civility Imprint

"Leila Awale is a fierce woman, a woman who ignites motivation wherever she goes. She is unapologetic about who she is and what she does. One thing I like about her is the fact that she doesn't pay attention to who dislikes her, rather uses that energy to embrace what her purposes are and goes on. For me, she has inspired me in ways that I cannot even explain, being a woman and from the coast, she has added onto my unapologetic attitude and when I see her I am constantly reminded of never being sorry of who I am and what I can bring to the table. She is a lady to watch out for because her vibe is infectious" -Nadia Ahmed, Founder FLO Author "The Feminist In Us"

"Her ability to entertain, inform, and educate all at the same time was key to the success of my event. She spoke with transparency and conviction allowing each audience member to not only see into her life but to reflect on their own life as well. She challenged them to demand more from themselves and to hold themselves to a higher standard. In the end, she connected with them on the head level and at the heart level.

Having Leila as a speaker at my Live Your BEST Life event in Nairobi took an investment. Her message and her presence delivered a magnificent return.

If you're looking for a speaker that will move your audience to take action, whether it be in a personal or professional manner, look no further than Leila Awale. She will deliver!"

-Dr. Ruben West

"As an Imprint Leader"

By
Leila Awale

My name is Leila Awale. I am a serial entrepreneur, life transformational coach, motivational speaker, women empowerment expert and a peace advocator.

Life is never smooth. They say it's a road of ups and downs but my life had all sorts of roads and plenty of turbulence but in the midst of it all as I look back now those were the roads that molded and shaped me to be the woman that I am today.

I was brought up in a culture where women's voices were stifled yet I rose up to speak and became a voice for the voiceless. Our culture did not encourage women to be in leadership positions, yet once again I took my place at the table.

Courage became my best friend when I was in Somalia during the war and that's when I realized if only the world had peace and no war. During the two years I was in Somalia, I knew I had to master all the courage that I had and at the same time cultivate humility. Courage to overcome fear during the war and humility to be able to spread civility and give hope to those that lost everything to the war that displaced families and created orphans. That took away everyone's livelihood and living.

From your nice bed to having no house to live in as its been bombed to ashes. I knew than that my calling has been found. I was there for several purposes.

Leaders need to learn to be humble and empathetic as much as they are courageous and strong. Especially now during this era, we must exercise civility at its highest.

My motivation has always been my father who taught me so much in life and always lead by example. And the other have always been my WHY…

Your WHY will always propagate you to accomplish, achieve and get through. Remember you grow through what you go through.

I run several companies and always advocating for peace and women empowerment. If there is one thing I get appreciated for, it is teaching all to remain grounded and standing no matter what life throws at you. At peace we avoid war. War within ourselves and with others. It is so important to remain calm during the storm. With civility meaningful communications are formed thus creating deep connections. Levels of understanding are met too.

"I am an Imprint Leader"

Glendora Dvine

Glendora has been a nationally accredited licensed counselor since 2007 and board-certified in Telemental Health since 2014. She founded Dvine Systems GA, a mental & behavioral health practice in 2010. Services to the community were provided face to face before COVID-19. Now counseling services are provided virtually via Telemental Health. Glendora has become recognized for her passion in 2 primary areas 1) Family safeguarding through healthy mental living 2) Coaching mental health professionals in the business of Telemental Health. Glendora started successfully coaching mental health clinicians in 2020 when she launched her mastermind program "Build. Scale. Grow. In Telemental Health," where she has facilitated clinicians in becoming leaders in their community and online through her branding systems, VCC, Glendora's VCC Systems has help clinicians understand the importance of being able to voice their niche, shine with confidence, and talk with competence. Glendora's system is founded on Visibility, Confidence, and Competence. Helping clinicians conquer the journey of entrepreneurship is Glendora's goal as their mental health professional coach.

To contact Glendora Dvine visit her website @ Dsgeorgia.com

Glendora Dvine LPC BC TMH
Dvine Systems GA
Licensed Professional Counselors
McDonough, GA 30252
Phone (678) 212-5146
Fax (678) 831-3554
www.dsgeorgia.com Facebook

Me Before Saying, "I do"

By Glendora Dvine

I am Glendora Dvine, a survivor of domestic violence. I was born in Detroit, Michigan and was raised there for the majority of my life. Summertime was spent in Heidelberg, Mississippi surrounded by cousins, aunts, uncles, and grandma. My childhood was uncommon because I was raised by my father alongside my two brothers and typically you will find a single mother raising 3 kids. By the time I was 16, my interest in the world outside my family had started to peak and I began working my first job at Burger King. I was proud of myself for having a job, my own money, and most importantly the ability to be outside of my house with my father's permission. My father was strict and never bent his rules. For example; I was never allowed to spend the night at anyone's home (not even a cousin's growing up). I always had to make sure his pants were ironed for work by the time he got up. I had to participate in an activity that he chose (cheerleading, basketball, piano). I think the worst part of not obeying my father was the loudness of his voice, the deepness of his tone, and his physical appearance of being angry (let me not forget the curse words). As loud and strict as my father was, I had never heard of a story or saw him raise his hand to a woman. He was married to my mother during the time my brothers and I were conceived. I had gotten confirmation from both of them as a young adult that he chose to raise us alone and allow our mother to continue to party in the streets freely and that is what she did. After my father divorced our mother, he married another beautiful being. This marriage was short-lived due to my father using her as a babysitter instead of a partner for which she never signed up for. Then there was his final marriage. In none of the marriages, I never saw my father do to those three women was what was coming my way. By the time my father married his third wife, I was in college. I was dating my first boyfriend that soon came to be my fiancé' after dating for five years. By that time I had met his aggressive behavior of cursing, yelling and screaming. I, like many women from the inner city, took on a persona of not being afraid to fight back. I found myself in the middle of constant yelling and arguing. Then he popped the question. Will you marry me? Not having a close relationship with my father or mother and being made to feel as if I didn't belong in my father's home by his last wife and her children was confirmation enough that I was supposed to marry him and follow him wherever he was headed. So I said yes, just as unsure as I was. I was unsure because I didn't like yelling, cursing accusations and screaming. I thought I was being smart. I would accept his proposal but schedule the wedding for two years out. Little did I know that two years went by so fast. Before I knew it, I had paid for an entire wedding damn near by myself with seven people standing on each side of us at the altar. The marriage lasted four years before I realized that I was living in a world that never was meant for me to be in.

I was raised in the church where I was taught about the goodness of God. I learned so many songs that sang the praises of the Lord and soon came to realize that is how I was staying sane. I found myself in the middle of a domestic hell hole. I was now married and living a nightmare. My husband had graduated from yelling and screaming to flat-out spitting in my face. I had never seen anyone spit on before and was too embarrassed, shocked and confused to tell my brothers or father. I found myself being accused of letting other men in our home and use his deodorant. I was the reason his truck had a flat tire even though I didn't drive it. I was always a name other than the one he stood in front of the altar and told God he was going to honor. Spitting leads to bruises on my arms and neck and the infamous words of no one is going to love you like me. One day praying, I asked God to show me a sign to know it was okay to leave the marriage. I noticed the sun was piercing through the window, shining on a book bag he kept. I went to the bag and opened it, finding a hateful letter that he had written about me. I was in shock at the words I read. The most hurtful and despicable words one after another all describing me. He had written his feelings out one day when he was angry at me on this paper in red ink. When I questioned him about the letter, he acknowledged it to be his true thoughts and feelings when angry. I struggled with leaving the marriage for four years because I didn't want to disappoint God. I didn't want to break my commitment to God. I believed God might punish me for leaving the marriage because I joined in marriage to honor God. After finding the letter, it became confirmation for me that relentless crying, being battered and abused is not how my God wanted me to live. I suddenly remembered how I lived spiritually before I met and married him. I remembered that my God is forgiving (it will be okay to end the marriage) and can see me crying in misery days on. I started to zone in on how I couldn't point out one man throughout my life that I knew of who physically and emotionally abused women. The next time was his last time because I left and didn't look back. I remembered that I was someone before him that was covered by the same Lord and Savior that covered my grandmother when she walked this earth. Being able to remember where I came from spiritually before I said, "I do," saved me from continuing a downward cycle.

"As an Imprint Leader"

By:

Glendora Dvine

I believe that a leader can learn from my imprint the importance of implementing spirituality and the importance of self-love.

Step one for leaders is to comprehend the importance of who they are serving and the behaviors they are doing to serve daily. Being mindful of how you carry yourself as a leader based on your spiritual beliefs can help continue on the path of leadership. Leaders who are spiritual reach a point in life that keeps confusion, ill-will, and other negatives of life a distance by focusing on the good that is in you for you and coming to you.

Step two is to intentionally take time out for yourself and teach others how that is a normal part of living. Too many times we run as humans in a circle trying to figure out what to do next or trying repeating the most comfortable patterns because of the fear of change. A leader doesn't fear change but embraces it with the understanding that difficult times are to come just like the times of laughter. Selfcare is taking care of your mental, emotional, and physical health by telling people "No", sitting alone, simply not talking, and finding ways to laugh out loud with others just to name a few. To be an effective leader, you must take time to wind down just like you take time to take care of others and work. A leader will always put their oxygen mask on first before helping someone else.

I hope to lead leaders based on my imprint to understand that personal development is inevitable and the quicker they realize it the quicker they will continue to enter into a peaceful mental and emotional state of life. My motivation to stay focused comes from my knowing that I am a generational curse breaker and covered by the highest, Lord God.

"I am an Imprint Leader"

By: Donald D. Toldson, Sr.

1. Just showing up is not nearly enough! You must show up intentionally, with purpose and to IMPACT. I show up to IMPACT in everything that I do. My Challenging Life Civility Impact started early in my life after my father was killed. I remember going to my fathers funeral. My older brother was in chaos, my Mom was in chaos. Even though I was sad, I found the courage to hold it together and comfort my brother and my mom by telling them that everything is going to be OK. I remember as I was growing up, my mom hit a rough patch in her life, she was depressed. I remember taking my money. I

am going to the store and I'm buying her a new Bible. It was all I knew how to do. She believes in God but she just needed some encouragement. I purchased her a new Bible as a symbol of the beginning of a new day. I showed up for my Mom to Impact her life as she began her new day.

2. Leaders can learn and lead based on my imprint simply by showing up with a purpose, be the example, be the Leader, be the one to encourage others regardless of how you feel or what you are going through. The person who has been my motivation to stay focused on my Civility Imprint as a Leader has been Sir Clyde Rivers Royal name HRH Okogyeman Kobina Amissah1. Even though he has been in my life a short period of time, learning about his life legacy has impacted me in such a way that it has caused me to stay focused as I lead by treating others with kindness and respect. He leads by being the example and it is impacting the world. My motivation is to live by the Civility Golden rule, " Treat others the way you would want to be treated, especially when you are

leading." Blessings.

-Donald D. Toldson, Sr.

"I am an Imprint Leader"

Dr. Onika L. Shirley

Dr. Onika L. Shirley is the Founder and CEO of Action Speaks Volume, Inc. She is known for building unshakable confidence; stopping procrastination, getting your dreams out of your head into your life, and helping entrepreneurs scale their businesses to 6-figures. She is a Master Storyteller, International Speaker, serves in Global Ministry, International bestselling author, International Award Recipient, Serial Entrepreneur, and Global Philanthropist impacting lives in the USA, Africa, India, and Pakistan. Dr. O is a Motivational Speaker and Christian Counselor. She is the Founder and Director of Action Speaks Volume Orphanage Home and Sewing School in Telangana State India, Founder and director of Action Speaks Volume Sewing School in Khanewal and

Shankot, Pakistan. She founded, operated, and visited an Orphanage home in Tuni India for four years and supported widows in Tuni, India. She is the founder of Empowering Eight Inner Circle, ASV C.A.R.E.S, and ASV Next Level Living Program. Dr. Onika is a biological mother, adoptive mother, foster mother, and proud grandmother to baby Aubrey and Kendalynn. She has served more than 12 years as a therapeutic foster parent for the State of Arkansas while also remaining extremely involved in her community. Of all the things Dr. O does, she is most proud of her profound faith in Christ and her opportunity to serve the body of Christ globally. Dr. O faithfully walks and serves in many capacities to make a difference in the lives of others. Dr. Onika volunteers throughout her community and abroad. She has served with great passion for many years. She has always been a helper and has had love for others that needs her help. She goes above and beyond when she knows she can be a blessing to someone else and actually move them from point A to point B.

Remembering the Obstacles I've overcome

By Dr. Onika L. Shirley

It's not always who, but sometimes what that challenges one to rise and lead courageously. The love for life and the desire to help as many people as possible all over the world is the ultimate goal of the legendary leader. My desire is to help individuals in every way possible to become aware of their true leadership potentials. I want to leave a powerful legacy long after my life here on earth is over. Remembering my own obstacles opened my heart of compassion for others when they're faced with undesirable life distractions. I remember early one Friday morning getting on the road after working 3rd shift 45 minutes away from home. I was a nineteen year old mother and a senior in high school. After driving for about fifteen minutes, I got really sleepy. I thought it would be a good idea to pull over and after all that was the agreement I had with my grandmother if I ever felt myself getting tired. After pulling over on a Piggly Wiggly parking lot, I checked the doors to make sure they were locked, I leaned back, and I went to sleep. After taking a nap for what seemed like enough time to get back on the road, I started back driving. I honestly felt like I was good to go, but was I wrong. After driving for another 15 minutes, the unthinkable happened. I fell asleep and I was driving on the wrong side of the road going head on with an 18-wheeler. The result of that impact was life changing. I went through 19 hours of surgery, almost two months in the hospital, physical therapy, and walked on crutches for an entire year. I had a long road to recovery. I had never seen anything to this magnitude in my life, but I had an early experience at the age of 10 that I feel in hindsight prepared me to deal with what I was going to have to conquer.

I was doing what most parents do. I was simply working trying to provide for my daughter and myself but I quickly went from being a healthy teenager, working mom, and senior in high school to a disabled unemployed mother. Charles Swindoll said life is 10% what happens to you and 90% how you react to it. I had no idea that what happened on March 22, 1996 was coming, but what I did know is that I had to deal with it. When I say I had to deal with it, I mean I knew that I would have to fight an internal battle for my healing. For me the healing process started on the inside. It started literally in my head; and it quickly came out my mouth, and into my life. I had faith that healing was mine even before I really understood what faith was. I just knew that God wasn't finished with me yet. I knew that my road to recovery was long, but I had the mindset that I was committed to doing what needed to be done to overcome this obstacle because my baby girl needed her mother. I also knew the leader in me had to resurrect, I had to be patient in my healing, and kind to others in the process. This was a faith walk. "Faith without works is dead" James 2:26 by faith, I accepted the power of God and trusted that He was my healer. The accident was tragic, but the greatest tragedy is not in having gone through something, but to live an unfilled life without purpose.

Without a doubt, we've all had something traumatic or negative to happen in our lives that caused us to experience emotional shock and the sting from it probably had you wondering if you would ever endure, much less see the good from it. I took my life changing experience and flipped it to be a blessing to others around the world. I wake up every morning excited to live because I didn't die that Friday morning. My survival was proof that I still had purpose. I had people to see, I had something to say, and had even more to serve. I believe that I exist to bring awareness to others as to why they are here. This is was not the time for me to be bitter but it was the time strive every day to be better. I now know that God's eternal gifts were awaiting me. God still had a great work for me to do so it wasn't over. It's now my life's purpose to help others to see that their life matters and that no matter what they go through that they have enough of what they need in them to keep going when life tries to stop them. Life will happen to the least of us, to the most of us, and to be honest at some point to all us. I believe with the right resources, strategies, and support we can overcome anything. You see purpose unfulfilled can't be stopped until it meets up with destiny. According to Ephesians 1:11 "Before we were even born, He gave us our destiny: that we would fulfill the plan of God who always accomplishes every purpose and plan in his heart." I believe that it's such a blessing to discover why we are here. It's also a blessing to impact the lives of others while knowing that some of those impacts will have lifetime impression. Your civility imprints will contribute to making the world a better place.

The 10% that Charles Swindoll was talking about is everything that life has thrown at you the problems, circumstances, and situations. But purpose fulfilled reminds us that our gifts, our skills, our talents, and our abilities can be used to respond to the problems, circumstances and situations in a way that works for us verses against us to create the life we want and the impact we need. In the process there will be obstacles. We always want to respond with love and kindness rather it be with actually people or with a situation that has happened in our lives. I started a strategy for my recovery. When we experience life changing encounters we must be strategic and we must be committed to our breakthrough. We can still be loving, kind, and patient with others and with ourselves. I promised myself that I would always be positive, I would keep moving even when it was physically painful, I would keep moving even when others thought I couldn't or shouldn't, and that I would not give myself permission to make excuse and today 25 years later I'm living the life of my dreams and helping others around the world. I help women build unshakable confidence, stop procrastinating, get their dreams out of their heads into their life, and leverage their time, their income and their impact. I want to make a big impression in the world by the works I have done and the words I have spoken, Action Speaks Volume. People will know where I have been and they know where I am going.

My dreams are big and I desire for the world see to it. I have opened doors of opportunities for individuals to embark upon the life of freedom they desire. Freedom that allows one to do more of what they love with the people they love with the added convenience of being able to do it from anywhere. I am a woman that went from working to receiving SSI disability to responding differently to my situation to now earning well over 6-figures. I'm leaving imprints by the choices I make on a daily basics. The quality of my daily imprint endorses and promotes others to choose similar paths to be better, to serve better, and to make positive impacts though out the world. The paths in our lives can be divine and only the individual experiencing the encounter can determine if there had been an imprint left in their heart to allow others to see new life imprints of God's amazing grace and his tender mercy by way of the their good to others and their impact throughout the world.

"When you reach an obstacle, turn it into an opportunity. You have the choice. You can overcome and be a winner, or you can allow it to overcome you and be a loser. The choice is yours and yours alone. Refuse to throw in the towel. Go that extra mile that failures refuse to travel. It is far better to be exhausted from success than to be rested from failure." ~ Mary Kay Ash.

As one overcome obstacles and they endeavor to share their experience with others it's vital that it's done with integrity, empathy, courage, and gratitude. As world leaders, we must become better leaders locally in our communities and abroad across the globe. We will become better leaders not only by what we say but by what we do. "The greatness of a man is measured by the way he treats the little man. Compassion for the weak is a sign of greatness." ~Dr. Myles Munroe.

Words to Live By from Dr. Onika

1. Remember you have never exhausted every option
2. Be open minded
3. Have self-awareness
4. Have faith that "This too shall pass"
5. You have to treat yourself like you matter
6. Don't allow your actions to betray what you said to you "Be your word"
7. Overcoming any obstacles requires both patience and urgency
8. People that has overcome help other to overcome " Leave your imprint"
9. Serve with a heart for God's people and love for God
10. Strive to be a leader that stands for change that benefits people for their good.

"As an Imprint Leader"

By: Dr. Onika L. Shirley

One particular challenging life impact that triggered me to Rise and Lead courageously was being raped at the age of ten by a public school teacher and hearing the words of defense to cover their part of opening the door for it to happen from others leaders in the school district. I learned early in life that sometimes you have to move differently and lead from a position of righteousness verses following the majority. Leadership is its basic form is two things: who you are showing up to be and how you are thinking about any giving situation without being bias to no thought at no time and for no reason. Leadership is about discovering your purpose in life and then becoming aware of the way that true leaders lead and think so you can fulfill your innate calling. My children has been my motivation to stay focused on my Civility Imprint as a LEADER. After experiencing a few life changing experiences, it was very important for me to understand who I was as opposed to what I do or what had been done to me. Only after understanding who I was I was able to take action naturally from the awareness of my leadership revelation. I believe I was born to lead and now I live and think like a leader. In order to think like a leader, I had to receive thoughts of leadership from my creator. It required a personal encounter to understand why I was here. I now understand that I have a leadership spirit and the spiritual of leadership and today I lead from a place of who I was born to be and not from things that happen to me after I was born. I am with Action Speaks Volume, Inc. 501 (c) 3

"I am an Imprint Leader"

By:

Dr. Karen D. Moore

    I was a beautiful melanated girl trying to fit in, trying to be excepted by the other children. I really wanted to be liked by the other kids so I wouldn't have to eat alone, be excluded from school activities. I wanted to be able to have lunch with this really cute boy, Johnny.

The thing is, I was not feeling beautiful, valuable or worthy after Johnny told me he did not want to eat with me because I was "too dark". I felt terrible because I didn't understand the problem with my dark skin. I felt even worse about the situation because I thought I had done something wrong. I felt like a confused, misunderstood girl.

I carried that feeling into my adult years until I read Psalm 139:14. I mean really read it to comprehend the full meaning of the text. The God's Translation version says, "I will give thanks to you because I have been so amazingly and miraculously made. Your works are miraculous, and my soul is fully aware of this." My soul became fully aware that I was made in the image of God. All of my beauty was attached to the creator of the Universe. I became aware of how amazing I really am!

I established I AM The Colour of Beautiful Global to address the hurt and trauma of colorism. I am inspired and committed to empowering deeply melanated women of color to embrace their power and beauty and walk into their destinies. Leaders must know who they are and empower others to discover the beauty and value that God has bestowed upon each and every one of us. As a leader, I live by my mantra We Say It Loud, We Wear It Proud! I Am The Colour of Beautiful! Grab ahold of your core belief and you can lead people to healing and deliverance!

Dr. Karen Moore Founder – I AM The Colour Of Beautiful Global

"I am an Imprint Leader"

Tamika Rowe

Tamika Rowe is a 42 year old United States Army Disabled Veteran. She served in the Army from 1996-1998 as a Combat Medic. She is the mother of five children, 2 daughters and 3 sons. She has faced many obstacles with her health after serving in the Army and had to medically retire and leave her career in Respiratory Therapy in 2007. After 12 years of battling with severe lung issues, Tamika relocated to Greenville, South Carolina where she became involved in many areas of community service. Despite the challenges she faced physically, she continues to persevere and is a very active member in her community serving veterans and those in need. She volunteered from 2016-2020 serving as a Policy Council member and Liaison to the Board of Directors for Community Action Agency Sunbelt Human Advancement resources (S.H.A.R.E.). Tamika was a Policy Council Representative that oversaw the federal policy, procedures and budget allocated to fund S.H.A.R.E. Head Start's Early Education program, birth-5 years, homeless services, youth leadership, and other community resources to develop low income families and improve their quality of life. She is the recipient of the 2019 S.H.A.R.E. Against All Odds Award for her service to SHARE while overcoming obstacles with her health, family and finances.

Tamika is a lifetime member of The Disabled American Veterans Organization (DAV). She has been elected to the position of 2nd Jr-Vice Commander in The Disabled American Veterans Department of South Carolina (SCDAV) 2019-2021. She is responsible for but not limited to community outreach and publicity for fundraising events to support veterans. She has provided food and toiletry items to Veteran Nursing Homes across South Carolina on behalf of SCDAV. Tamika is also the DAV National Deputy Chief of Staff Representative for South Carolina for which she advocates for the needs of Veterans on behalf of their National Commander. She has hosted the 2020 Women Veterans Day Celebration in recognition and honor of her comrades in Greenville, SC. Tamika is a certified Veteran Disability Claims Officer and volunteers her time assisting Veterans complete and submit disability compensation claims, retirement benefits applications, surviving spouse benefits and more. She has been involved in assisting veterans locally and across the state of South Carolina since 2018.

Tamika has volunteered her time to be a mentor to local veterans who reside in the Transition Facility for Homeless Veterans. She provided mental, spiritual and financial coaching for the veterans. She also provided them with monthly steak dinners to celebrate their lives and boost their morale. Tamika has had success stories with her mentees, which are now building their own homes, starting master's degree programs while becoming self-sufficient and living independently. Tamika also volunteers her time serving with The Upstate SC Quilt Of Valor Foundation (QOVF). She received in 2019 a Quilt of Valor Award for her honorable service in The Army. Quilt of Valor is the highest award a veteran can receive from a civilian. She is now a facilitator of Quilt of Valor Ceremonies in the Upstate of SC. Tamika coordinated a historic First All-Female Veteran Quilt of Valor Award Ceremony in Greenville, SC in February of 2020. Tamika founded The Upstate South Carolina Women Veterans Group in 2019. The group meets monthly to provide a safe place for women to share their experiences, network, receive emotional & spiritual support, camaraderie, friendship and gifts of appreciation. The Women Veterans group has veterans who served in Vietnam, Afghanistan, Iraq, Germany and many other locations. Tamika has received the 2020 I Change Nations International "Women Add Value" Award for the work she has done in the community with veterans. Tamika is the 2021 recipient of the Sister Veteran Service Award for her service to the community.

Tamika is a Minister with the Redemption Pastors Fellowship since 2019. She provides daily devotionals, prayer and encouragement to the Redemption Church community as well as through her personal Facebook page since 2014. Since 2016, she has volunteered as a teacher in the Redemption East Coast Children's Ministry on Sundays. Tamika continues to serve her veteran comrades and members of her community with integrity, faith, compassion and empathy. She strives to help as many people as possible to improve their quality of life and fulfill their purpose.

Against All Odds
By Tamika Rowe

"Being confident of this very thing, that He who has begun a good work in you will complete it until the day of Jesus Christ" Philippians 1:6 NKJV.

We all experience challenges in many different areas of our lives. I experienced a series of traumatic and life-changing health conditions that have impacted my life for the past 24 years. At age 17 while serving in the United States Army, I developed a lung condition that has changed my life forever. I was only a teen with a promising future in the Army as a Combat Medic but after only two years of service, I developed a lung condition which led to difficulty breathing and I was no longer able to perform my duties and so I had to be honorably discharged. Even though I felt like a failure because I was not able to finish a career in the military and retire, I found hope and confidence because I was able to attend college on a full scholarship from the Veterans Transition Program and obtain a Bachelor's Degree in Biology and Medicine.

Things don't always go the way I had planned. I felt like everything was working against me, but I began to meditate on this scripture and it has helped me focus and persevere through all the difficulties that I have faced over the last 24 years and now help to encourage others who experience difficult situations "We are troubled on every side, yet not distressed. " We are perplexed but not in despair, persecuted but not forsaken, cast down but not destroyed.", Romans 6:8-9.

I am an Army veteran that enlisted my senior year of high school at age seventeen. I had no idea how my life would change drastically after only serving two years in the military. While serving in the Army, I developed a lung condition that would later cause me to be discharged because I could no longer carry out my duties as a medic. After leaving the army, I received my Bachelor's degree and was employed working in

Respiratory Therapy. I worked as the chief clinical technician for two years and due to exposure and allergic reaction to a drug, I became severely ill. Since I had pre-existing lung damage from being in the Army, the exposure to a chemical I was using frequently at work had a negative impact on my body and I became disabled. I was recommended for medical retirement and was placed on social security disability for the rest of my life. I was only 28 years old and a single mother of 3 children one of which was only a few months old. Little did I know that this was only the beginning of 12 years diminishing the quality of my life.

"God has a purpose for your pain, a reason for your struggle and a gift for your faithfulness. Don't Give Up!" -author unknown

I was very discouraged and confused about this new stage in my life. I was experiencing challenges in my physical body that I had treated patients for, but I never expected that it would ever happen to me. I was a 28 year old suffering from severe Asthma, Chronic Obstructive Pulmonary Disease (COPD) and Emphysema. I was taking high dose steroids, nebulizer treatments every four hours and a host of other medications just to stay alive. I had 24 hospital admissions in one year because of several exacerbations and difficulty breathing. My life was a mess and I was struggling to take care of my children and myself. I went from making over $40,000 a year in respiratory therapy to barely making $1,200 dollars a month on social security disability. I really thought that things would never get any better as the doctors told me that my condition would continue to deteriorate over time and that I would die at a very young age. Things went spiraling downward quickly and I became crippled from the waist down and was confined to a wheelchair by age 29. The steroids I was taking to keep my lungs functioning have caused some myopathy and neurological conditions in my legs and I could not walk. I spent almost a year in and out of rehab facilities trying to regain strength and feeling in my legs but I didn't make much progress. This was a very difficult time in my life as I was separated from my 3 young children and I could not care for them like a normal healthy mother would. The church I attended at the time stepped in and helped to take care of my children, clean my home, and many other things to make sure I had the best quality of life possible. My condition was not improving and my doctor recommended that I relocate to a place with warmer weather since I was wheelchair bound and the harsh New York winters were making it more difficult for me to breathe and travel. I was under a great deal of stress physically, emotionally and mentally but I persevered and made plans to relocate myself and my 3 children to Florida.

Starting over is never easy, but when it's a life or death situation you make every effort to adapt and overcome it. I'm grateful for the resilience training I received in the army as well as my foundation and belief system, because without that I would have not made it through the big transition and relocation to Florida. After 2 years of suffering with debilitating Asthma, COPD and Emphysema, I had no other choice but to pack up my children and start a new life in South Florida. I had a 9, 5 and 2 year old when I relocated. It was a struggle being a single parent severely disabled with limited income and resources trying to raise 3 children. I had my Father and my faith. Within a few months of relocation, I started walking using a walker to assist me to travel short distances. Through much prayer and hard work, the muscles in my legs had miraculously regained strength and I was able to start being active in the church singing on the Praise Team and teaching the New Members Class. I had beaten the odds and overcame everything the doctors said I couldn't and wouldn't ever do again. They told me I would never walk or sing again and that I would be on oxygen for the rest of my life. I thought that my life was taking a turn for the better and I finally had a chance at a normal life with my children again. After about a year of being in Florida, I started experiencing excruciating and debilitating pain in my hips and it was difficult to dance, get

out of bed and sometimes even walk. I went
to the doctor to get evaluated and found out
that as a result of taking high dose steroids
consistently for many years, the bones in both
my hips became totally necrotic and died and
I would need to have bilateral total hip
replacements. My whole world seemed to
come crashing down once again. The muscles
in my legs had recovered from the steroid
damage but my hips were too severely
damaged and required surgical intervention.
There I was, 30 years old and about to start
the transformation into becoming the bionic
mother as my children would call me.

**"No virus can stop God's plan for your
life"-author unknown**

It is never easy when you have to
encounter unexpected physical changes in
your body, especially when surgery is
involved, but I learned to trust God and
confess His healing and promises for my life
every step of the way. So there I was ready to
have a total hip replacement surgery. I was the
youngest patient the surgeon had ever had for

this procedure and before me he had only read about my condition in textbooks. This definitely didn't make me feel any better but I trusted God and I was going to do whatever was necessary to improve my quality of life and be there for my children. Surgery was a success and after only two weeks I was back in church, singing and dancing on the praise team, teaching classes and giving God glory for my healing. Two years later, I had the second hip replacement surgery and I recovered quickly then too. I amazed the doctors and everyone that I encountered by my resilience and drive to be and do better. Since I wasn't working and my income was limited, I decided to start a small home daycare to help some friends that were in school by taking care of their children day and night shifts so they can advance in their careers. I charged less than the normal daycare would so they could save for school, books and more. I wanted to help those younger than myself get a chance of a better life knowing their children were being taken care for. I am so proud to know that these women are doing great things now because I took the time to help them even when I needed help myself. I learned that it is important to help others when you have the ability, opportunity and resources because you are making a deposit, impact and imprint on future leaders. It made a difference in their lives because I cared and made it easier for them to attend school without worrying about the safety of their children. It made a difference in my life when I decided to live unselfishly and show compassion and empathy whenever given the opportunity and help improve the quality of life for others when I can. I lived for about 3 years with stable lung conditions and only a few hospitalizations for breathing exacerbations. I finally thought I was experiencing a somewhat normal life again and then I had a relapse.

When you think you have overcome all the health obstacles and then you're hit with another even more serious problem than the previous, what do you do? You dig deep into the foundation of your belief system, surround yourself with faith filled people, make daily confessions that lineup with your goals and you don't give up. After living what I considered to be a somewhat normal life, my lungs took a turn for the worse and I relapsed. I went from 75% lung capacity to 25% and I was declining rapidly. The doctors put me on 24 hour supplemental oxygen and told me I didn't have much time and that I didn't qualify for a lung transplant so I needed to get my affairs in order and find someone to care for my 5 children. This was the most devastating news I have heard in a long time. I became severely depressed and isolated myself from family and friends. The only real source of inspiration and life I had was coming from my church pastor and members in South Carolina, Bahamas and a few other countries. I shared with them my dilemma and they prayed with me. The depression was so bad that I decided I wanted to die because I didn't want my children to see me suffer much longer. I decided to remove my oxygen one night so that I would just pass away in my sleep. I knew this was not the Christian thing to do but I was overwhelmed and not in my right mind. Early the next morning about 2 am, my oldest son came down stairs, saw I was turning blue and he connected me back to the oxygen and that was the beginning of my second chance at life. Later that day, I repented before God and called my pastor. She prayed with me and assured me that this was not the end but only the beginning of something beautiful. A year had passed and I gradually began to improve in my lung condition. I still required supplemental oxygen but I was no longer homebound and my life was heading in a positive direction. I made a decision that in order to continue to improve my health and quality of life, I needed to be in an environment of faith, accountability and support. So I started my journey to transition and become a South Carolina resident.

Here I was at one of the most pivotal moments in my life and I had no idea what to expect in this new season of my life. I was moving to a state that I had only visited a few times before, a place where I had no family and I would be starting all over again. I knew the transition would not be easy, but I was confident that this was a God move and that He would give me everything I needed to make this transition successful. After living in Florida for 8 years and having so many ups and downs physically, emotionally and spiritually, I was ready to start fresh and leave everything negative behind. When I arrived in South Carolina in 2016, many different things were happening in my life all at once and it could have become overwhelming but I had a great support system with my Redemption church family. Things were changing quickly and I had to make the best of the new circumstances and help my children adjust as best as I knew how. I was still using supplemental oxygen therapy, but overall my stamina and quality of life was improving closer to normal over the past year. I went from being at death's door to being an important part of my community as a servant leader.

Many different health obstacles came against me continuously for about 12 years, but finally I was in a place where I could make a difference and serve again in my community. I was no longer in a wheelchair, I wasn't stuck at home strapped to an oxygen tank and I could breathe fresh air again without struggling or fighting to catch my breath. It was not an easy task getting off the supplemental oxygen, but I was determined to have a better quality of life. I enrolled in an 8 week intensive Pulmonary Rehab Program and after completing the classes, I had developed enough capacity and stamina to come off supplemental oxygen. This was the beginning of a new chapter in my life. I got my independence back and I was determined to help anyone that I could to do the same. I enrolled my two youngest children into a Head Start Program and began serving on their leadership panel as a volunteer representing low income families, helping them improve quality of life and find resources to rise above poverty. I finally started to live and dream again. I felt like myself again after almost 9 years and I was finally able to get out into the community and serve again. I served with S.H.A.R.E. Community Action Agency for 4 years as a

Policy Council Representative and Liaison to Board of Directors. While serving on the team, I learned many leadership skills and was exposed to multiple community resources that helped me and many others improve our quality of life. One year after serving on the policy council, I became completely debt free, purchased my first ever brand new car and bought a 4 bedroom, 2 story house. I was living out my dream, surviving against all odds. My story was presented to a panel and I received the Against All Odds Award in 2017 for overcoming all my health issues, rising above poverty and serving in my community. This was an opportunity of a lifetime. I was serving and learning with such influential men and women who encouraged me to do and be better and to never give up no matter what I faced.

"In order to leave a legacy, you must first live one." -Ruben West

In 2018, I joined the Disabled American Veterans Organization which helps empower and equip veterans with disabilities to file for compensation benefits and gain access to a better quality of life. Within a year, I was elected to a state level position as 2nd Jr Vice Commander for the Department of South Carolina Disabled American Veterans. While serving in this capacity, I donated food and toiletry items to veteran nursing homes, homeless veterans and families in need. I served as a mentor to homeless veterans in transition homes as a spiritual, social and financial advisor. I assisted the veterans in creating goals, writing budgets, gaining access to community resources, praying and other needs. Recently one of my mentees has acquired a brand new home mortgage free, and another of my mentees is building a new home from scratch. It has been an honor to serve in this capacity, because I know what it's like to be the veteran with limited income and disabilities that impact quality of life. I was recognized for work that I was doing in the community with veterans and others. I was nominated and received a Quilt of Valor Award in 2019. I joined the Quilt of Valor foundation and now I serve as a representative in Upstate South Carolina that facilitates the Quilt of Valor Ceremonies for Veterans in our state. I hosted the first all-female Veteran Quilt of Valor Ceremony in Greenville, South Carolina February, 2020. The volunteer services that I provide for veterans have led me to network and collaborate with some very influential people.

I founded The Upstate South Carolina Women Veterans Group in summer of 2019 to bring together women veterans in a safe place to share life experiences, provide camaraderie, network, fellowship and gain access and knowledge to community resources. This group has veterans from the Vietnam Era to current active duty and reservist. We are located all across the upstate, but we come together to support and encourage one another to navigate life situations. Since I started this group, I received the 2020 I Change Nations International Women Add Value Award and the 2021 Sister Veteran Award for the work I do with women veterans and other veterans in the community. It is my desire to equip, empower and impact as many women that I can to leave an imprint on the next generation. I also donate monthly to the Lamb Professional Basketball Scholarship, which was founded by my Army comrade to help empower and sow into the lives of our future leaders. I received the 2021 Lamb Professional Scholarship Award for highest Monetary Contributions. When I think about where I was financially a few years ago and where I am now, I know that it is only the goodness of God why I have what I have. He gave me a desire to serve and lead unselfishly and that is what I will continue to do. I appeal to you, that if you are in a position to volunteer your time, give financially or be a listening ear to someone, please do so. Because you never know the impact you can have on the life of someone just by being there. I knew that my life was spared for a reason and I was going to use this second chance to make a difference in the life of someone.

I thought the battle with my health was resolved or at least stabilized but then came something else. I started to have severe pain in both my shoulders before I relocated from Florida. However, I was not in any condition to have any surgical procedures, so I was prescribed pain medication for the necrosis or bone death process that began in my shoulders as a result of long term steroid use for my Asthma and COPD. I decided to see a doctor because the pain was unbearable and was affecting the quality of my life. The prognosis was not good. The bone in my right shoulder was completely dead and started to collapse and the left shoulder was not too far behind. I was disheartened, but I knew what God did for me when I had the hip replacements and how quickly I recovered. So I just knew this too was going to be easy. We scheduled the surgery for January of 2018, everything went well and as far as they knew there weren't any complications. Two days later my situation took a turn for the worse. I was having difficulty breathing and chest pain. After a few diagnostic studies, the doctors realized my lung had collapsed and my diaphragm was paralyzed. This was a side effect from the nerve block and should have resolved itself within 24hr. Well, in my case it was getting worse and they were considering putting me on a ventilator and only gave me 2 days to live. I called my church family and they prayed with me and I believed that I would survive yet another attack on my life. It took 5 days but finally my diaphragm started to return to position and my lung began to expand again. I was discharged home after 6 days on bed rest. When I returned for a follow up a week later, all issues were resolved and I was back on the road to recovery. The surgeon scheduled my next shoulder replacement for 6 months later that year.

The second shoulder surgery was less complicated and I only experienced temporary paralysis of an eye and that resolved after a few days. I thought I was in the clear and well on my way to recovery, but 6 months later I got into a car accident and damaged my newly replaced shoulder. The surgeon did a second procedure to try to fix the damage to the shoulder, however after extensive physical therapy the shoulder was not functional and I had to repeat the replacement surgery, this time with more parts and my shoulder had to be reconstructed. Finally, surgery for my new shoulder was a success and with a few adaptations and a cadaver graft I was well on my way to life as usual. Well that's what I thought. One week after surgery, my legs started to swell and I was experiencing shortness of breath. This continued for a few days, but got to the point where I decided to get help. I went to the emergency room and test results revealed that I had right side heart failure and a possible blood clot. I was like… God really, how much more of this can I take. I was reassured in my spirit that the weapon had formed but it would not prevail. I called on my prayer team of pastors and they were in agreement with me that all would be well. After 24 hours of treatment with medication and observation, over 7 pounds of fluid was released from around my heart and lungs and I was on my way to recovery. The doctors, who told me the day before I may only have 5 years to live with heart failure, were now telling me that they see no sign of heart damage or blood clot. That is the power of prayer and confession. One week after discharge, I was driving with one arm in a sling to see clients processing claims and resume my normal duties.

I know the God that began a work in me will finish it and though I may have been cast down, and almost destroyed in my body multiple times, God always made a way and Healing prevailed. I have overcome all the obstacles that came up against me and you can do it too. My suggestion to you on how to overcome is that you define what it is that you believe and solidify the foundation of your belief system and values. Find books and other resources that help develop you as an individual. Make a plan for your life, establish short and long-term goals. Establish relationships of accountability and equity with similar goals and beliefs, cut off toxic people, create an environment conducive for growth and peace. Redefine and establish good character traits, study who you are and who you want to become. Make daily confessions and journal entries towards your desired goals.

If you desire to impact others and leave an imprint on their lives, then you must network with others that share your strengths, align yourself with persons who can help you develop and refine the areas of your weakness. Serve to help others reach where you are trying to go be it community service, or volunteer opportunities. When you have reached your desired goals, start mentoring others teaching your strategies to overcome. Continue to feed yourself with healthy reading, videos and fellowship. Maintaining a good character environment without compromising your values and belief system

"My triumphs are proof that I do not live in fear, I live in faith"

"As an Imprint Leader

By: Tamika Rowe

It is my deepest desire that the next generation of leaders learn to recognize and fulfill their God-Given potential. I aspire to awaken their awareness that we are all made in the Image (Character & Nature) of God our Creator. We are also created in His Likeness filled with His potential and wisdom walking in dominion (Genesis 1:26). I intend to be a part of this next paradigm shift which transitions followers into leaders that walk in dominion and authority given to us by God our Father. Our father in Heaven is legacy minded and so He sent His son Jesus as a seed so He can have many sons, and so I intend to inspire and impact leaving and imprint of kingdom identity, authority, character and leadership qualities with biblical foundation as well as practical life experiences. Dr Myles Munroe and Apostle Ron Carpenter Jr have been my inspiration and very instrumental in transforming my mindset to that of the kingdom of Heaven. They have taught me to walk in character and dominion and exercise my heavenly citizenship right while on earth. I intend like my mentors to "die empty" Myles Munroe and in doing so help others to maximize their potential and leadership capabilities. I am a Minister with Redemption Ministerial Fellowship under the leadership of Apostle Ron Carpenter Jr. I am also an affiliate with I Change Nations Founded by Sir Clyde Rivers Royal name HRH Okogyeman Kobina Amissah 1.

"I am an Imprint Leader"

By:

Celeste Purdie

Successful leaders tap into a special place within to give them a slight edge. This special place is known as the internal compass. Learning to follow your inner compass will always lead you to success that is for you. My background is a United States Air Force veteran and a 25-year veteran in the Human Resources industry. I used all those skills that I learned and used to survive and build a great career where I could lead and teach skills to others to be successful. After leaving Corporate America, I used some of those very same skills to transition to entrepreneurship successfully. Some of the essential skills I use daily include:

1. **<u>Service</u>**. Finding a way to be of service to others. The more people I serve, the more successful I become. Helping others allows you to organize, plan, teach, coach, and delegate skills vital for successful leaders.

2. **<u>Joy</u>**. Look for opportunities that bring you immense pleasure that you would want to do even if you did not get paid to do them. I have found that when you are passionate about something, and you wake up excited to engage in activities related to the things that bring you joy that eventually you will master that action, and the money will follow! Do not chase money, instead pursue those things that bring you joy!

3. **Competition**. Look in the mirror and recognize that your biggest competitor is staring you in the eyes. Always look inward to find ways to be more

successful. Routinely ask yourself; are you focused on beating your best, improving your skills, practicing self-development, critiquing your quality, and asking others for feedback to help you improve.

4. **Curiosity**. Being curious about everything has been a skill that allows me to stay focused on the strategy versus getting caught in a narrow, tactically focused mindset. Leaders who have great success know that the intersection of concepts is where the magic typically happens. Thus, ask questions to find out how ideas and those concepts might be related, fit into the bigger picture, or be used in another manner to promote breakthroughs.

5. **Relationship**. Finally, leaders develop honest and genuine connections with people, so get curious about people that you meet. Great leaders connect people in their network to other people that can be helpful. Think of you being a sponsor for bringing great people together. Always look for

opportunities to sponsor and grow your network. When you genuinely are curious about people, you find out so much about what they do and the value they bring to your community. Try being fully present with the next person you encounter one-on-one by eliminating distractions and listening to them.

These skills provide a compass for me and help me leave a leadership imprint. These same skills are transferrable to other leaders, and during my years of career coaching when I was in human resources, I would encourage leaders to strengthen their skills in these areas. As an entrepreneur, I remain focused on sharpening these skills as I know my past success as a leader comes from these fundamental skills, and the better I get at them, the better I become as a leader, making an imprint!

Celeste Purdie
www.Purdieinc.com

"I am an Imprint Leader"

Yemi Sekoni

Yemi Sekoni, is the president of Donahue Models & Talent, LLC - Rhode Island's oldest and most successful modeling agency. Her company books some of New England's top professional models and talent and works with many corporate giants across the region, helping these companies to launch successful advertising campaigns and convey critical marketing messages.

A recent graduate of the Goldman Sachs 10000Small Businesses program, Yemi has a bachelor's degree in education, a post-graduate diploma in marketing, and an MBA, and has worked in banking, relationship management, event planning & management. She has over 40 years of experience in various areas of the fashion and entertainment industry, including theater, TV, film, print and runway.

Civility Imprint

In addition to running her agency, Yemi is the founder and creative director of Rhode Island Fashion Week, and the host of Fashion Fete, a virtual fashion & beauty series and designer consortium that provides consulting, educational and business support services to fashion designers with the mission of helping them develop and grow their own design businesses

Believe In Yourself And Work Hard. Dreams Do Come True.

By Yemi Sekoni

I firmly believe that what Ms. Betty says about the only thing that stands in someone's way is themselves is true. Hello, dear readers! My name is Yemi Sekoni. I'm half Jamaican, half Nigerian; born in the UK. I do a number of things, but first and foremost, I own a modeling agency. I work with companies in the local market that my agency is in, which is on the east coast in Rhode Island. My company provides models and talent for various marketing and advertising needs. I work with designers for my models, for their fashion shows.

Alongside that, I also produce Rhode Island fashion week. Producing fashion week means that I am providing a platform for local fashion designers to feature their latest collections. Of course, with the pandemic last year, the lockdown happened, so we didn't get to do that.

I say that the business word of 2020 should have been "pivot"! Because if you speak to anyone in the business world last year, the word "pivot" was always in the conversation somewhere. I did a slight pivot during quarantine and in place of producing a fashion week I started to host a virtual fashion and beauty series that features designers and their collections from all over the world. People would tune in from anywhere in the globe and watch the shows and learn a little bit more about fashion in another part of the world where they didn't really have any knowledge of.

Acting is another passion of mine since I was probably five or six years old when I did my very first play. I was in *The Sound of Music*. Strange as this may sound, I remember distinctly the moment when I heard the opening song "The hills are alive with the sound of music." As the music played, I was conscious of a thought in my head that said, "This is what I would do for the rest of my life." This was it. At that point, I didn't really know what that meant. It's just now years later, when I think about that moment, because I never forgot it. It made sense.

I started in school plays when I was in grade school. In my family, that set me apart because no one else shared my same passion for performing but it's just what I was meant to do. My mother was an admin, my sister's a pharmacist, my brother's an engineer, and my dad was in insurance, so everybody did something different. And then there was me. Thank goodness my mom never tried to quell that artistic side of me, this passion that I had. So, whatever the school play was, mom would always come and see the show.

All the way through grade school and up to when I was in college, I was studying. I got my Bachelor's in education, but with a minor in fine art. I was always in the drama department. Most of my friends were in drama. Every time they had an audition, I was auditioning. So I was always in the school plays. I also sung in the band. I'm not a great singer, but I also sang in the band at school. The performance aspect, that side of me, it's such a huge part of who I am, and it's impossible to separate.

I moved here from the UK in in 1999 and then I moved to Rhode Island in 2001. When I settled in Rhode Island, I started to really want to get into the industry here and I didn't know where to go to talk to someone about it. So I just kind of asked around, telling people what I did and I was working at the bank at the time. One of my colleagues there said, "Well, I don't really know anything about the industry, but there's a place called John Casablanca's. Why don't you call them up?"

I don't know if you're familiar with John Casablanca's, but they teach modeling classes and they've got locations in different states. So, without knowing what they did, I just went and set up an appointment. I explained to them that I was an actress. And they were like, "Well, we don't really do acting here, we do modeling. We're modeling school."

So, I decided to sign up and take the modeling program, but I wasn't thinking of modeling. It was just kind of odd, you know, something maybe that's helping to get my foot in the door, and then hopefully I'll be able to get onto the acting side of things. But then I realized that modeling was so much fun and I started to pursue that.

Then I joined Donahue, my agency, as a model back in 2005. At the time, I didn't realize that the head of the company had been looking for someone that she could groom to take over the agency because she was looking to retire.

She liked my energy, my passion, my personality and my hardworking nature. So she started to mentor me without me realizing that was what she was doing. Around 2009/2010 after about four years of modeling for the agency, she approached me and asked me if I'd be interested in buying the company from her. And that's basically what we did!

I've done a little bit of everything: theater and independent movies. I never got to be featured in a major movie but I've done background work. Had I not taken over the agency, I probably would have gone on to pursue the modeling and acting a lot more. But my role changed and I have been a leader for 11 years.

When you get to do your day job and that job is what you're most passionate about, it never feels like work. Each and every day when I get up, I'm in charge. I'm always grateful that I am doing what I do because it's enabled me to really make this a full-time career. Whereas most people in my local market do this part-time, which is what I was doing when I was actively modeling and acting, something else had to pay the bills. Still, it has been wonderful to be featured in commercials and TV shows. It's always cool when I get an email from someone who says "Oh! This looks like you" when they open up an in-flight magazine on the way to Jamaica. It happens very often and it's cool. I get a thrill every time.

Now, let's talk about inspiration. There have been lots of inspirational figures in my life. Whenever people ask me who inspires me, the first person I think of is also the first person I considered an icon. That person is Denzel Washington.

Set aside the fact that he's gorgeous, it's much more than just his looks. I remember him saying in one of his books that, from an early age he wanted to be known first as an actor then as a person of color. That's not to say that he was trying to diminish who he was as a person, but he didn't want his ethnic origin to be the sole definition for his talents. He's a phenomenal actor and really looks to be cast in roles that aren't dependent on a character trait, because that was something where he had no control over. He was who he was and so he wanted to just be accepted for a human being who could act.

From the get-go, I thought, "Wow, that's pretty cool." As a person of color and I don't want to get political here, I know that everybody has had an experience where, because of the shade of your skin tone, something has or has not happened. Some of us grew up or have grown up with a mindset that because of that one trait, it may limit us from doing the things that we should be doing, or we don't go after this because we don't think they're going to accept us because we look or sound a certain way.

My mindset has always been: I don't care. I don't wake up in the morning thinking "I'm black." I'm just myself. This is what I do, and I just want to do it. My philosophy is, if I try to do it over here and the people don't want to play with me, great. I'm just going to build my sandbox elsewhere and do my thing there. With that mindset, I find people that want to play in my sandbox. I don't need to waste energy or time on people that don't want to play. I ain't got the time. I've got stuff to do! So, Denzel was my very first inspiration.

My next inspiration was, of course, Oprah. Enough said. One thing in particular that Oprah said really resonated with me. I happen to have been working one night and she was on TV and I wasn't really paying attention, but out of everything she said one sentence came out of the entire conversation that seeped into my consciousness. I'm paraphrasing here but she said, "Whatever you do, do it to the utmost. Do it as though somebody's watching, even though nobody's watching. Always do your best because you never know who's seeing you and who's watching you."

That's been a mantra that I've also lived by. As you can probably tell from my energy, I'm always operating at like 120% because that's who I am. I never believe in doing something halfway. Either do it a hundred percent or don't do it at all. I commit to things fully because I'm feeding my soul. I'm doing the things that I enjoy doing and I want to be able to, when I'm on my death bed, look back at my life and not have any regrets about what I did or didn't try or fail to do because I was too scared. So, I just throw myself into it a hundred percent and I enjoy myself. I have fun doing what I do.

The third most inspiring person is our current Vice President, Kamala Harris. If you watched when President Biden was giving his first annual message, I just happened to look up at the television and I honestly didn't even see Biden in the middle. I just saw Nancy Pelosi and Kamala Harris on both sides. You couldn't even see their faces; all I saw were the pearls, the camisole they had underneath, and their blazers. I thought, "Oh, God, is that a picture or what?"

That moment for me was just incredible. I've never subscribed to "I cannot." Again, I believe that the only person in your way is you. But the fact is in that moment, a lot of young girls, regardless of their ethnic background, could look at that screen and not question whether or not they could be in those two positions of power. A lot of us grew up in a time where women were still regarded as second-class citizens. Now we're beginning to see a transition where we're really instilling it into young girls that they can do and be whoever they want to be.

To quantify what I said, that I have never subscribed to thinking "I cannot." That is unless it's something that does not align with my personal philosophy. I don't just say yes to everything that crosses my table. I have to make sure it aligns with something that I would want to do. However, if it's something I set my mind to, that I want to do, then I intend to do it. I love a challenge. Even if I don't know how to do it, I still commit to getting it done. I face the challenge head on and ask, "How do we do this now? What's the challenge and how do we make it work?" I derive satisfaction from doing those things and I enjoy the process of overcoming those obstacles.

To finish my chapter, Dr. Betty asked me to define what resurrection means to me. Resurrection can mean a bunch of different things to a bunch of different people. Now, if you are religiously minded you're probably thinking of it in terms of Jesus Christ. He died. He resurrected for our sins. On the other hand, for those that aren't necessarily religious, it could also mean asking yourself "Where are you right now?" Are you in a place where you're happy? Sometimes, even when you're in a place where you're happy, there's always something new, something better, some next level you know, whether it's financial, emotional, intellectual or physical that you might want to aspire to. So you never want to think that you've arrived.

When I think back to 10 years ago, when I bought the agency, it was aside from the fact that yes, I had a business degree. I had an MBA. So, I understood the theory of starting a business, but did I have experience starting a business? No!

In order for me to get up and go to work and get this done and not have a heart attack, I told myself that I did not own this company. I worked for it. I cued it up for the first year also when people met with me for the first time and they say, "What do you do?" I would say, "Oh, I work for a modeling agency." I didn't say I owned it because I could not wrap my head around the fact that I had actually done that. Like, oh my God, what did I just do?

I was what, 41 or 42 at the time. I had support from my family and whatnot, but there wasn't a significant other, there wasn't somebody that I could come home at the end of the day and say, "Oh my God, honey, this happened today." As a result, whatever I was dealing with, whatever challenges I had when I came home, it was like, just me, myself and I. So, I was having that conversation with myself. There was no sounding board to share my thoughts with at the end of the day.

Now, 10 years later when I see where I am and my conversation, my dialogue, the confidence that I that I convey, I compare it to that young 40 something year old. I'm 52 now, just in case everybody's wondering. That young bright-eyed, bushy-tailed, woman, I can see that there was a resurrection that happened, for me. I had grown out of where I was, and I emerged as this new person. It's not just that I've emerged, but I'm now working confidently in the space that I am who I am and I recognize this.

I don't take myself too seriously. Life is too short, so I don't walk around like the Queen of Sheba, I'm just Yemi. I also mentor about five or six young business entrepreneurs, ones that are coming up now, because I feel it's nice to be able to give back and give a hand to the ones coming up behind you. One of them is very young. When he first connected with me, he said," I didn't really believe that you existed, that I would actually get a call from you. I cannot believe I'm having a conversation with you right now". He was totally awestruck and I'm sitting there thinking, "Oh, you need to just sit down and talk to my friends who will say that Yemi is just Yemi."

Having said that though, I do recognize the persona that people see on the outside. It took me a while to get there. I said my resurrection is going from where I started 10 years ago to whom I am now and it's constantly evolving. In another 5, 10, 15 years, when I'm about to retire, who am I going to be at that point?

So, as individuals, when we're thinking about growth, personal growth, that's something that we should constantly be thinking about. We're moving from one spot and we're emerging somewhere else. It's like a snake hole. You know, the animals that shed, you shed, that key thing, whatever that is. It doesn't need to be physically. You know of course I'm not talking about your skin, but the beliefs, the thought process. A lot of us live by that "I cannot" or this is holding me back where I couldn't do this because I'm not tall enough. I'm not old enough. I'm not whatever, I'm not whatever the limitations we put on ourselves. Instead, it's about putting that part of you to rest. There's nothing wrong with that. We have to go through that in order to be able to go out of it and come into the next stage or next version of who you want.

Just like I am constantly shedding, we are all constantly shedding these experiences, but those experiences combine and make who we are. You cannot separate, and you shouldn't regret. You should not be apologetic for who that person was five years ago, 10 years ago because it's part of your learning process. You have those battle scars and you wear them proudly. You keep them with you so that you can share those experiences with the young people coming up so they know that they too are going to resurrect. Part of the experience that you're giving to them becomes part of their experience as well.

If there is just a piece of wisdom that I can leave you with as a takeaway, it's that life is too short. Don't think about it. Do it. Wise men once said, "Don't talk about it. Be about it."

Don't talk. Talk is cheap. A lot of us tend to talk and we don't always implement. Don't let grass grow under your feet. So, if I make a decision to do something, I start to think about ways to get it done. You eat the elephant one bite at a time, not all at once. So, whatever it is, you set your mind to do baby steps every day. It will be done before you know it. You're going to be looking back thinking, "Oh my God, I've accomplished it!"

Don't talk about it. Be about it.

"I am an Imprint Leader"

By:

Vernet Alin Joseph

Productivity is a beautiful way of life that can be challenging if you are not ready to produce in life. The lack of productivity means there will be a lack of effectiveness and efficiency within whatever arena it's missing that you are dealing with. There are several questions one must ask themselves daily. Are you willing to fight for what you believe? Are you truly hungry enough to seek what you dream of above all else? Well that's the mentality of extremely productive people "FIGHTING" is what it's all about. Sometimes you have to fight yourself, fight mediocrity, fight procrastination and fight normalcy to gain what you want. Everybody wants success but not many people are willing to fight for it. Extremely productive people rise and lead courageously because they live their lives to the fullest. Here are 5 P's to leaving a productive legacy imprint:

1. Purpose - to fulfill your assignment and be the best version of yourself.

2. Preparation - in your distress there is always a lesson.

3. Pain - learn to endure the agony and make it count.

4. Process - is the road through to your destiny.

5. Progress - is the road to your growth. Here is an extra nugget for life application.

A = Action with Anticipation (Forward Thinking))

C = Creativity through Collaboration (Study Groups)

T = Target Transformation (Set Goals That Will Stretch You)

NOW = No One Waiting "Dr. Vernet is helping organizations like yours get Fixed, Focused, and Dedicated to the cause of increased productivity!"

"I am an Imprint Leader"

Dr. Betty Speaks

Dr. BETTY SPEAKS is retired with HONORS from the United States Army, 2021 I Change Nations Global Newcomer of The Year Honoree Giving birth to "The Resurrection Imprint Act," an award winning I Change Nations International Speaker, Global Network Virtual Marketer and Entrepreneur, 8x Best Selling Collaborated Author, Jesus Woman at Godheads Ministry, Ambassador to the Pink Pul-Pit International Ministry, Intentional Mastery Story Teller, Certified Black Belt Speaker plus she has been featured on TV shows and a host of Radio broadcasting. When Betty Speaks... she Speaks Dr. BETTY SPEAKS is that power voice for those silenced by (traumatic situations throughout their journey in LIFE). Her mission is to help others who have (remanences of their experiences) destroy the silence and SOAR. Her transparent story of (grief, depression, and healing), along with my strategies for the inspiration to SOAR, will help them to know they can do the same. As a World Ambassador and a genuine leader to all she encountered, she realized that she needed to be the first to speak out so she can effectively inspire others to SOAR. A global leader, a global executive coach, and an international author; She have devoted her influential voice to Podcasting a phenomenal global show "Overcoming Battles by Being Strong and Courageous" A Life Change Now Plus featured on the Power of Praise Network every Sunday at 3pm!

Inspiring others to SOAR with H.O.P.E
> **S.O.A.R** Seize Opportunities and Rise
> **H.O.P.E** Help Other People Enjoy Life
> **S.O.A.R** Seize Opportunities and Refocus

Realizing that "Strength doesn't COME from what you CAN Do; It COMEs from OVERCOMING the things you once thought you CULDN'T."

Dr. Speaks is your Life IMPRINT Leader! She is extremely passionate with empowering individuals to establish themselves through the four components of LIFE (Spiritual Growth, Financial Literacy, Personal and Professional Development). She's that chosen warrior who inspires others to create an IMPRINT that will live on long after they're gone.

Readers can connect with Dr. BETTY SPEAKS
www.bettyspeaks.com : Facebook:
https://www.facebook.com/betty.speaks.92
Instagram: https://www.instagram.com/bettyspeaks

Chapter One

Find Your Leaders

Photo by <u>Jehyun Sung</u> on <u>Unsplash</u>

Much is said about Leadership, a spirit of Leadership and really the ability to lead. Companies are increasingly looking for people who know how to lead. It is not possible to learn Leadership in articles or simply take a PPT or PDF presentation of Leadership and develop to master a good leader's techniques.

Many talks about coach leadership and

political Leadership, but what do you mean by Leadership? Does management leadership have an impact on the techniques you seek to use? What is Leadership in the company where you work? What types of Leadership can you identify?

What is leadership

Photo by Markus Spiske on Unsplash

A good leader must first understand the idea: Leadership can lead a group of people and turn them into a team that produces results. In other words, a leader has the skills required to inspire and influence followers ethically and constructively so that they can willingly and enthusiastically contribute to the team's and organization's objectives.

However, leading is a complex task, since to be a good leader, you need to have technical skills to manage employees and the team, but, besides, it is also necessary to have the ability to develop your team members, meeting personal and professional expectations, aligned with the interests of organizations.

The importance of leadership

Companies that have or develop leaders within their nuclei tend to achieve success.

The leader has great importance in the processes of any organization. He is someone who wears the company shirt and becomes the company himself.

Leaders are still linked to people management and are responsible for passing on the company's philosophy and engaging the team so that the organization's task, vision, and values are matched with the team's way of working.

As a representative of the organization, the leader must fully understand the company, knowing how its sectors and processes work. Furthermore, the involvement of Leadership in various centers provides the organization with continuous input on how the goals are progressing and a higher level of communication with its employees.

Types of leadership

Photo by Matteo Vistocco on Unsplash

There are different types and Leadership.

Each of them is special and works according to the organizational environment in which they are employed. Having a specific leadership style does not mean that others are wrong, but it is always necessary to adapt to the team's environment and needs.

The type of leader directly impacts the performance and results of the team. The way of leading influences the behavior of everyone around you. As a result, if you are dissatisfied with your actions and strategies or have not yet found yourself within the organization and are looking to develop new skills and Soft Skills, it is important to know each of the types of Leadership. Are they:

- Autocratic Leadership;
- Situational Leadership;
- Democratic Leadership;
- Liberal Leadership;
- Transformational Leadership.

In each type of Leadership,

1. Autocratic leadership

Autocratic Leadership involves absolute and authoritarian control over a group. This style of Leadership is defined by the leader's complete control over all decisions. In autocratic Leadership, he has little reference to the opinion of team members when it comes to autocratic rule.

The characteristics of autocratic Leadership are:

- The leader determines the measures and techniques for carrying out the tasks;
- The leader determines which task each one must perform and which one is his / her work partner;
- There is no promotion of the team's effective participation in the projects;
- The leader alone makes all the necessary decisions and usually oppresses his subordinates;
- The leader does not value subordinates' skills, knowledge and results;
- Exerts excessive collection, causing some discomfort;
- Limits the performance of the group.

2. Situational leadership

In situational Leadership, the leader adapts to certain situations. In other words, to exercise it, it is necessary to measure the team's maturity and the situation found to develop the best leadership style for the group.

There is a link between Leadership and management in this form of Leadership. The leader needs to frequently evaluate his employees and change their leadership style, leaving him dynamic and flexible. Seeking to use different models of performance according to the situation found.

The characteristics of situational Leadership are:

Direction: the leader supervises the task until its end, directing the employee to elaborate it until gaining confidence;

Orientation: the leader contributes by supporting the acquisition of new ideas and disseminating knowledge when the employee needs help;

Support: the leader is responsible for encouraging the employee to acquire security and seek learning, increasing their skills and knowledge;

Autonomy: the leader maintains contact with little supervision and little support.

3. Democratic leadership

In this type of Leadership, subordinates are all involved in business plans, policies, procedures and goals, facilitating discussions and increasing productivity. The democratic leader needs to get involved, discuss and monitor the teams. Besides, in this type of Leadership, both work and decision-making are done in conjunction with subordinates, always listening, guiding and driving the team.

The main characteristics of democratic Leadership are:

The leader encourages and helps to make group decisions in all activities plus, encourages the realization of plans and achievement of objectives.

The leader leaves the direction of the

work to the choice of the group. The guidelines are discussed by the group, encouraged and assisted by the leader;

The team outlines the steps and techniques for reaching the target, requesting technical advice from the leader when necessary;

The division of tasks is at the discretion of the group itself, and each member is free to choose his or her coworkers;

The leader seeks to be a normal member of the group.

4. Liberal leadership

In this way of leading, the leader allows total freedom for decision making. With that, the individuals or the group can decide and request to participate of the leader only when necessary.

Liberal Leadership offers more freedom to individuals in the execution of projects. Besides, the leader is seen as a facilitator of the process, being responsible for transmitting the information and stimulating the members' creativity.

In this way, non-constant supervision allows people to have greater responsibility for the project, and the leader is the agent that transmits information. With this type of Leadership, it is possible to assess the subordinate's behavior, level of knowledge, skill, commitment, and responsibility.

The characteristics of liberal Leadership are:

Subordinates are free to set their plans and goals.

The leader rarely gets involved in discussions, giving his opinion only if asked, interacting superficially.

There is freedom for group or individual decisions, with minimal participation from the leader.

The community has complete control over task distribution and companion selection.

The leader does not attempt to assess or

regulate the course of events.

The leader only makes irregular comments about members' activities when asked.

5. Transformational leadership

Transformational Leadership is characterized by the presence of a leader capable of transforming the environment and changing the environment's reality. In other words, a leader capable of solving problems from the simplest to the most complex. The transformational leader is usually visionary, strategist and committed to the development of his followers

In all areas of activity, transformational Leadership can change behaviors and training better professionals and people. Through his examples and attitudes, the leader serves as a positive reference, whose approach to dealing with individuals, bridging differences, and producing results is a source of motivation and inspiration for the entire team.

In this type of Leadership, the leader has the power to cause an exceptional effect on his followers, who start to be concerned with development, changing the way of thinking, always looking for improvement.

The characteristics of transformational Leadership are:

Charisma: the leader involves people and wins the collaboration of the team to accomplish what was proposed. With clear and effective communication, it promotes changes and achieves the cooperation and engagement of its followers.

Inspiration: with their examples, deeds and attitudes, the leader becomes an inspiration for the professionals under his management, becoming a positive reference;

Intellectual stimulation: the leader promotes intelligence, rationality and careful problem solving;

Individualized consideration: treats each employee individually, accompanies and advises.

Characteristics of a good leader:

Photo by <u>Dylan Gillis</u> on <u>Unsplash</u>

1. Self-knowledge

The first important characteristic is that of knowing how to guide you. This is not an easy task and whoever manages to do it soon becomes a point of reference for others, a leader in the eyes of those who do not have this ability.

It is also part of self-knowledge to know how to manage one's emotions and put aside unproductive emotional states, such as fear, insecurity, depression, anxiety, and stress, when they become an obstacle. These states are emotions with specific meanings, which cannot have space in certain situations.

2. Team spirit

Taking responsibility for a group seems like a basic task for any leaders, but this is not exactly what happens in practice.

Some leaders are the first to point out their team's flaws. However, a successful leader must find ways to resolve crises before distributing blame.

3. Have decision-making power

Another important characteristic of a good leader is the power of decision. The idea that we are the total of the decisions we make in life is a thought that should be the guide for a person involved in decision-making because only then is it possible to be aware of the consequences of a decision.

When a person understands the need and the importance of making good decisions, he naturally optimizes his decision-making power.

4. Good relationship

Usually, a leader participates in a group, where there are other leaders and other teams. The ability to create positive relationships is what differentiates a leader, as this demonstrates his ability to create bonds and attract people to himself and the ability to listen to team members, allowing him to act in a manner consistent with shared principles.

5. Versatility

The leader must deal well with changes, understand, and look for opportunities that provide the necessary vision for his business to grow. Versatility is a great competence that motivates, inspires, energizes and creates leaders capable of having a 360 ° view of various subjects that may compromise their day.

Other characteristics of a good leader

When we talk about Leadership, it is not enough to just want to lead. For this task, somewhat peculiar characteristics are needed that need to be developed. Generally, a good leader has the following attributes:

dynamic; creative; charismatic; proactive; ethical; communicative; inspiring; innovative; embrace challenges; good relationship; intuitive; empathetic; motivating.

To find your employees already in your company, you need to talk to your employees and analyze their routine to finally identify the characteristics mentioned.

How to find new leaders?

An option to find new leaders is through organizational management. It is a way of evaluating the points mentioned above, observing, and understanding its employees' profile.

Organizational management allows a broad view of the performance and development of those who are part of your company. With this information, human resources teams can identify individuals' leadership traits to create career and development plans.

How to develop organizational leadership?

Organizational leaders must have different attitudes when it comes to developing and working with their team. For this reason, organizational Leadership is developed almost daily. However, some tips can help in this development process.

1. Have good communication and transparency with the teams

Employees must be aware of the company's strategies and the real directions that the company seeks in its scenario. This is important for the leader to better identify with his organization and engage with his teams to align with the company's expectations.

2. Act with equality: avoid differentiating professionals by hierarchical level

A leader listens to his team in the same way, without giving preference to higher levels. A good leader places himself on the same level as other employees and values the different views and opinions, giving everyone openness to participate in the processes. Generating a better relationship between the teams, with greater confidence and less fear.

3. Seek to listen to the team: take note of problems and points for improvement

The leader must observe his team and see the possible difficulties and the ones that are already happening to ensure that the failures are corrected and motivate the professionals involved.

And the combination with keeping a close eye on your team for potential issues, you can recognize the strengths and improvement of each professional and assist when necessary to ensure a better performance for each one.

The first role of the leader

Although leadership has often taken on different meanings in different places and times, it is almost universally recognized that the role of the leader is to help oneself and others do the right things.

It is said that "a manager makes things do well, while a leader turns on the enthusiasm necessary to do them", thus recognizing in the leader the primary role of guide, of the one who traces the path, which shows the way to his team or organization.

The leader is first of all the person able to build an inspiring vision for others.

Let's be clear, in companies, the role of the leader does not end by "setting the direction" and then waiting for "something to happen" as if by magic, management skills are also (and a lot) needed. "A vision, without an adequate plan of action, is simply a hallucination", however, the primary role of the leader - even in companies - is to inspire others and guide them towards challenging goals. And if he does it quickly and efficiently, then the leader is also a good manager.

Leaders must, first of all, know the team dynamics, be an example and indicate a direction. They must then ensure, as managers, that team members have the skills and abilities necessary to do their job and realize the vision. Leaders must also regularly give and receive feedback on the progress of projects and provide the group with all the training and coaching tools necessary to improve individual and team performance. All this is the work of a leader within a company that intends to carry out "businesses".

PERSONAL GROWTH QUESTIONS

1. What do you understand by leadership and its importance?
2. Types of leadership?
3. Mention the main characteristics of democratic leadership?
4. What are the attributes to develop an organizational leadership?

Chapter Two

TAKE ACTION

Photo by Nick Fewings on Unsplash

I'd like to ask you a basic math question.

Five frogs are perched on a log.

Four of the frog's plan to leap. How many frogs are still alive?

Did you want option 1?

Still, 5 is the right answer. This is due to the distinction between determining and acting.

Have you had some personal experience with this? We have a propensity for making a lot of choices. We decide to eat healthily, pursue a higher education, or start a new company. Both of these decisions, though, are meaningless.

We must take steps for a decision to be meaningful. Although this idea is so basic, most people never go from agreeing to doing. They do not develop the habit of taking action and therefore do not achieve everything that they might. If we cultivate the habit of putting ideas and decisions into action, we will be better positioned to achieve the results we want.

"The convictions turn into feelings; your thoughts turn into phrases; your words turn into acts; your actions turn into behaviors; your habits turn into values, and your values turn into your destiny." –Anonymous.

Tried-and-true methods for moving from decision to action:

Photo by Kamil Pietrzak on Unsplash

1. Stop waiting for ideal circumstances.

You will wait an eternity if you wait for everything to be fine before getting started. There will never be an ideal situation. There will always be something wrong, or that could be improved. There is no such thing as a perfect time; there is just the moment. You must act right away, and you can make changes as you go. Last year was the ideal time to get started. Right now, is the second-best moment.

"Twenty years ago, the perfect time to plant a tree was. Now is the second-best time." -Ancient Chinese Proverb

2. Come to a complete stop, get up, and do it.

Decide to start acting. A man of action is someone who has an idea and acts on it right away. Have you ever told anyone, "It's a beauty second-best beach trip," and then sat in front of the TV? Stop, get up, and do it again the next time. Do you want to start working out or propose a new concept at work? Do it right now. We lose the will to step forward when we pause and wait, allowing anxiety to creep into our minds.

"The most difficult part is deciding to act; the rest is all tenacity." Amelia Earhart made history when she became the first woman to travel solo across the Atlantic Ocean.

3. Quit second-guessing the decisions.

Analysis paralysis paralyzes us when we overthink stuff. We start to over-analyze things to the point that we can't move on. We worry about how imperfect the situation is, question the amount of time we have available, or make various reasons for not taking action.

4. Make it a habit to take action daily.

Once you've gotten started, keep doing what you're doing. Keep the momentum going by doing something useful and important to your idea every day. Setting aside 15 minutes every day to complete a small task is a good example. Those small tasks will quickly add up, and seeing your work completed will help you build confidence.

"As long as you don't hesitate, it doesn't matter how slowly you go."

5. Take action to relieve your apprehension.

The overwhelming majority of people despise public speaking. Have you given much thought to the worst-case scenario? It normally takes a long time to speak. At this point, even the most composed and confident speakers may become nervous. Fear and anxiety, on the other hand, fade away once you get started. Taking steps will assist you in overcoming your fears. Become a doer and see what you can do to conquer your doubts and build courage if you're afraid.

6. Pay attention to the current situation.

The actual time to plant a tree was twenty years ago, according to the poet. in the words of an ancient Chinese proverb Now is the second-best time." Yes, we would have a fully grown tree offering shade right now if we had planted those seeds 20 years ago. If we don't plant the tree now, we'll still be standing in the sun in 20 years. Consider what you should do right now.

7. Remove any possible distractions.

If you have ever sat down to write an essay only to be interrupted by emails, social media accounts, or other distractions? or web searches? We live in a world that is getting noisier by the day. This noise can cause disturbances, hindering productivity and leading to procrastination. If you concentrate and block out distractions, your output will increase.

The simple truth is that putting one common idea into action is much more successful than saving 20 brilliant ideas for a later date or the ideal moment. Get into the habit of behaving when you have an idea or need to make a decision. Take a chance and see what great things you can do.

"It's much more effective to put an ordinary idea into motion than it is to save twenty brilliant ideas.

8. Visualize the long term

"The authoritarian is an insecure person who masks behind power. The modern leader works as a team, aware of the synergy and creativity of team / team work. To this end, it seeks to develop its team members, using and valuing behavioral training as an extremely valuable tool for personal, group and organizational development. In addition, of course,

Do you know how to motivate the team by exercising effective and coherent leadership? Continue reading and find the best way!

What is motivation?

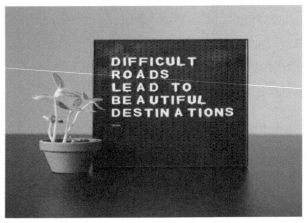

Photo by Hello I'm Nik on Unsplash

Feeling motivated brings countless benefits to the individual (both in personal and professional life). When we are stimulated to do something, we gain inner satisfaction that contributes to raising our self-esteem and well-being and increasing willpower, self-determination and individual competence.

Having well-defined goals and goals in life and at work is essential to keep up with this sense of engagement. Even better is when we find a purpose in life, which makes us see positive results in the short and long term.

When it comes to the professional realm, unmotivated employees are a danger to any company's success. In addition to gradually decreasing their productivity level, they end up negatively influencing the rest of the group.

This factor can compromise business results, opening up chances for layoffs and moments of crisis. But the good news is that a situation of isolated or systemic demotivation can be reversed when you have a leader who seeks to encourage and encourage employees with punctual attitudes, starting with their self-motivation.

How to become a motivating leader?

Photo by Nathan Dumlao on Unsplash

There is no greater chance of stimulating the team than working with someone who directs and guides the group's goals with motivation and enthusiasm. Remember that team members are the mirror of your leader.

However, showing enthusiasm in speech and actions is not enough to keep employees engaged, especially in times of difficulty and challenges. The following are some essential attitudes for you to become an example of leadership and motivation in your company.

Stay motivated

Okay, it's true that you, as a leader, should be the first to show self-motivation to your employees. However, for this, the attitude must be sincere, "come from within", and appear naturally in all your actions.

One such tip may seem self-evident, but it is all too typical for people in high positions to have issues with their employers or continually reconsider their personal and professional goals as if they are unsure about the path they want to trace.

When you are not genuinely motivated, work ends up being impacted. In the case of leaders, a domino effect is created, which leads the team to develop the feeling that it is not worth engaging with the company.

If this is your case, reflect on your position and whether your dreams and goals align with the company's goals.

1. Join the team

To become a leader that adds value and deserves to be followed, whoever is in charge needs to join the team, get to know each other's dreams and, as best as possible, stimulate their achievements.

It is necessary to look at the employee's reality, act with humility and justice, and place oneself in the position of "friendly shoulder" when necessary. But this must be done without losing the leadership and respect that the position requires.

2. Powered by Rock Convert

However, when approaching the team, it

will be possible to maintain a good relationship with its members and let feelings of trust and collaboration flow. At the same time, you can develop projects that align the company's global objectives with employees' achievements, keeping motivation high.

3. Develop the ability to manage people

To remain integrated into the team and encourage the best in each one, it is necessary to develop the capacity to manage people. The leader must learn to balance personal desires with professional goals and, above all, know how to map the profile of each one to understand who will be better at each task.

In addition to increasing the environment's enthusiasm and showing that you care about the team, you make employees believe that that organization invests in human capital.

When looking to improve people management, the consequences are:

- Improving productivity
- Retaining talent

- Development of new skills
- Ability to act strategically to find solutions in times of crisis

4. Offer individual support

Recognizing each one's individuality and talent is not enough to stimulate the essential qualities to achieve satisfactory results. It is important to respect the employee's nature, highlighting their strengths and providing individual support to overcome their weaknesses.

It is also essential that compliments, feedbacks and, mainly, criticisms are communicated individually and in the most appropriate way for each profile. Thus, gossip or maladjustment between team members is avoided.

Such a posture also contributes to reducing misunderstandings and feelings of inferiority, which can demotivate and take away the focus of the group on organizational objectives.

5. Create the culture of feedback

Great leaders usually keep their teams up to date on the role of each one within the company, their results and the points that need to be improved. This should occur not only at monthly meetings but constantly.

When he acts like this, the leader gains the confidence and tranquility of the group, increasing the motivation in search of a better performance of all. Therefore, it is very important to create a culture of feedback to have clear guidelines on the work performed and the goals that need to be achieved for better results.

6. Delegate tasks

Among the most effective ways to keep team members stimulated is to work on their autonomy by encouraging opportunities for growth and the creation of new skills.

To do so, decentralizing actions and delegating tasks according to each person's profile and competence shows that the leader trusts in the work of subordinates. Besides, it helps to establish healthy relationships in the workplace.

Distributing activities is also an excellent process for optimizing production. Do not forget that the accumulation of leadership responsibilities ends up overloading those in charge, hindering the sector's entire progress.

7. Set challenging goals for the group

Other factors that can destroy a team's motivation are routine and lack of professional challenges. If the employee starts to perform tasks on autopilot, it is up to the manager to create more challenging goals and activities to get him out of his comfort zone at an almost bureaucratic pace.

It is necessary to observe the profile of each one and understand who likes to feel challenged. However, in general, giving new tasks to employees is a good way to develop other skills, generating more self-knowledge and raising self-esteem.

PERSONAL GROWTH QUESTIONS

1. What are seven tried-and-true methods for moving from decision to action?
2. Ancient Chinese proverb states that twenty years was the perfect time to plant a tree, what do you understand by this statement?
3. How can you quit second-guessing the decisions?
4. What are the things possible distraction can lead to while moving from decision into action?

Chapter Three

FORM A COMMUNITY

Photo by Jed Villejo on Unsplash

How to build a community that resists any situation

What for many Boxes has made it possible to overcome the lockdown without major problems and return to business without particularities is the small community that every Box Owner has been able to create around their Box?

However, aggregating people with common interests is one thing; creating a community that can last over time and overcome difficulties, remaining compact, whatever happens, is another and requires the knowledge of some "mechanisms" of the base.

Communities will dissipate as quickly as they were born if neglected. They need nurturing and dedication from their leaders and their members through traditions, behaviors and knowledge sharing.

Today I am talking about these "mechanisms" that contribute to making a community solid in every situation, such as the international one of CrossFit, which, in addition to resisting attacks of all kinds, transcends the field of fitness and borders on the social and political movement. In short, I'll explain how to build a community.

Advantages of building communities

By associating with groups of people, you are interested in and profiles and habits related to your business, companies have multiple benefits for being close to your persona and working in a community that is already open to dialogue and form bonds. The following are other benefits of building communities:

Encouraging collaboration between people

Photo by Priscilla Du Preez on Unsplash

More and more, we notice the growth in the culture of collaboration and sharing, and this is very present within communities. The search for collective empowerment and the strengthening of the group makes this attitude diffuse in the community.

In this logic, companies should act as partners, as sources of solutions for the most diverse demands of the customer - who, in turn, feels more motivated to publicize their brand and the experiences lived in the community, creating a great collaboration and incentive cycle.

Increased transparency in relations

Trust is a vital factor for the full development of relationships in the community. In addition to strengthening ties, this makes people more comfortable expressing themselves, seeking what connects with their essence, and so on.

Likewise, it encourages a more transparent exchange with the other members, making the actions more solid and the results more fruitful.

Stimulating the feeling of belonging

As members interact and engage in a collective goal, the tendency is for the community to become even more associated with the group to feel responsible for its success and forties to be strengthened.

This feeling of belonging can be very beneficial for organizations because, in addition to generating a perception of customer value concerning the brand, there is a real partnership and genuine engagement of this audience.

Sharing of goals

Photo by taylor hernandez on Unsplash

In response to the seasons, about 1,800 of the world's 10,000 bird species migrate long distances each year. Many of these migrations are north-south, with animals feeding and breeding in the high northern latitudes during the summer and then migrating a few hundred kilometers south for the winter. Some animals use this technique to migrate every year between the northern and southern hemispheres.

A community's mission starts when its members decide to work together towards a common goal. The real challenge is to devise ways to involve stakeholders in such a way that new possibilities emerge. People are more likely to come forward if the aim has a sense of urgency to it. The subject or task must be important enough to inspire genuine dedication and must have a long-term goal, such as creating a better world together or assisting people in improving their lifestyles.

This reason for defending or pursuing a common goal must also be consistent with individual self-interest, whereas the added benefit of teamwork must be obvious to everyone. This common care becomes a bond of identity when the target is a mutual passion for nourishing the soul. Finding people who share your enthusiasm and mission is energizing.

The danger here is that an all-encompassing social goal can become "all for all" in practice. Society could become disconnected from the rest of the world.

A distinct personality

The Shuttered - also known as the civic guard or city guard - was a Dutch protective, military protection system for local civic authorities. Its officers were appointed by magistrates and were affluent residents of the city. Members were responsible for purchasing their equipment, which included a weapon and a uniform. The concept was that three out of every hundred residents belonged to the shuttered.

A culture sees itself as separate from the wider society in which it resides in some way. He may even have an adversary, a force against which he fights or from which he must defend himself, resulting in a "us versus them" situation.

This is the "globe gym" case, too often identified as the enemy to fight. However, many enemies that a fitness community can take sides against are mainly related to the lifestyle of the people in society or their habits.

To define their distinctive character, communities develop and promote common languages, rituals, symbols, moments and stories. This results in a shared culture that allows the community to act together.

Most groups are selective about who they admit: only those who share their passion and mission, as well as their qualities and values. Members of the community feel happy, honored, and fortunate to be a part of it as a result. What members like more and more about their society are the people.

The lifecycle of members ranges from recruits to novices, regulars, leaders, and elders. Each member is responsible for recruiting potential community members and helping recruits make their way into the community. Early in their life cycle, community members share ritual-rich experiences to immerse themselves in the community's culture.

Celebration is an important part of the

common culture that creates an opportunity to bond together and build deep trust. Communities celebrate new members, highlight community achievements and other key events, and recognize their leaders and elders' contributions.

Society is essentially characterized by shared ownership, enjoyment, and accountability. Everyone is treated as an owner, an investor, and a partner, resulting in a genuine sense of belonging.

A method of operation

Photo by Nastya Dulhiier on Unsplash

The Red Cross issued patterns for sweaters, socks, mufflers, fingerless gloves (which allowed soldiers to keep their hands warm while filming), mattress covers (for use with a cast), and other clothing during World War II. Survival patterns show that these knitting patterns were typed and reworked with carbon paper copies and shared between the jerseys. Many sweaters have chosen to repeatedly knit the same garment in the same size so that they can memorize the pattern and produce pieces more quickly.

The joint action is where the community's magic lies. Members of the group find each other, collaborate, help one another, and achieve success together. This is the satisfaction of doing productive work with like-minded individuals, with colleagues.

Communities have a collective intention, however tacit and distributed, to administer their specific domain of knowledge and support learning about it. Therefore, communities promote the curiosity, learning, and professional mastery with which all community members are guided, with quality content.

They offer a learning partnership: continuing education through peer-based learning, facilitating courses or providing knowledge to members. They organize information flows, useful links, joint problem solving and knowledge creation. This results in lifelong learning.

Communities depend on their members' financial contributions. This is not a "recognition of the value earned" or a "check for services rendered." Instead, it contributes to advancing the common good, strengthening society, and distributing the wealth produced.

A safe location

You'll need a good foundation to create a safe house. When the Amish community needs a new house or a barn built, men come from miles around to assist.

Communities include a haven, a place to

celebrate, and a place to congregate. This location is lovely, comfortable, and worthy of showing off to tourists. The house's architecture reflects the community's culture, values, and history. In this case, we're about the Box.

Being a part of a family provides a secure environment: what happens within stays inside. Members of the community are mindful of the delicate circumstances in which some work and value each other's privacy. In the outside world, the group supports its members, and they can depend on one another for shelter, help, and access. Since its members may be nomads, the group requires something portable and light: a life tool that allows them to remain linked even when separated physically.

A digital platform works as a reflection of the health and vitality of its community. Online practices can mimic offline community experiences: introducing new community members, sharing knowledge and resources, news and announcements from members. Users and members are also protected online and know that the conversation is monitored and sometimes guided by community facilitators and members.

Events that take place in groups

Which better way to nourish both your body and your soul than to share a meal? The picture of a big Italian family eating lunch together on Sundays at a long white table dressed as a table in the garden is one that we can all relate to.

The importance of celebration and interaction cannot be overstated. Throughout the year, communities plan activities such as a major annual festival and many smaller regional events. These encourage people to interact in real life, facilitating real-life interactions. As much as what to commit to, it's important to know how to commit to things: How societies bring people together is just as critical as the substance of what they share.

Let's bring it together.

These broad characteristics can be extended to a wide range of cultures while remaining distinct entities that encapsulate our modern environment. Their leadership style may also classify communities: some have a single figure who leads the rest of the community, while others share full control over each position, allowing them to self-govern in a more stable atmosphere. This collaborative effort ensures that the project can last longer and stop imploding, often the case.

Tips on how to develop your company's community in a strategic way

It is not sufficient to necessarily join any groups to form communities. It is important to examine its goals and determine how to improve results strategically and collaboratively. As a result, keep an eye on the following factors:

- understand how to entice talent
- empower the people in your neighborhood

- build a relationship of trust with the community
- Let go of what isn't producing results.

Consumer behaviors on the internet, especially on social networks, necessitates the creation of communities in which affinities, shared interests, and collaborative relationships can be found, including with businesses, given that consumer-brand relationships are becoming closer and more humanized.

Besides, brands and other institutions such as the family and the state play a role in the public imagination.

Organizations that recognize this phenomenon and incorporate community building into their strategic planning have stronger consumer relationships and, as a result, greater organizational and financial performance.

PERSONAL GROWTH QUESTIONS

1. How can you build a community that resists any situation?
2. What are the events that take place in groups?
3. How can distinct have impact in personality?
4. Enumerate the purpose of sharing goals?

Chapter Four

PEACEFUL TRANSITIONS

Photo by Cameron Venti on Unsplash

The importance of good Leadership for companies to succeed and remain successful is undeniable. As a result, there is a lot of work. On the part of the companies, for the development of the leaders. Although the assignments for leaders vary according to each organization, three experts argue that there is a common path that all professionals need to follow to become ready for positions of command - what they call Leadership.

The importance of good Leadership for companies to succeed and remain successful is undeniable.

Transition 1: from managing yourself to managing others

The first transition is usually from individual collaborator to top management. It makes professionals learn to plan work, assign tasks, motivate, train, and measure others' activities. In other words, there is a change from "doing the job" to "having the job done by others".

According to the authors, the big problem is that this transition does not follow a change in behavior and values. According to Ram, "these changes will only occur if top management reinforces the need to change beliefs and if people feel they are successful in their new jobs after a change in value."

Action plan to achieve your goals

Transition 2: from managing others to managing managers

The biggest difference between the second and the first transition is that professionals need to completely detach themselves from individual tasks. On the other hand, mastering selection skills are required to identify those who will go through "transition 1," allocate managerial work to them, track their success as leaders, and provide guidance.

Managers must also begin to look beyond their immediate duties and consider strategic issues that impact the whole organization at this stage.

I n practice, many companies promote these positions to employees who have not gone through transition 1. This may prevent them from learning to value managerial work. As a result, they hold frontline managers accountable for technical work and promote employees according to technical potential rather than leadership skills. The authors consider that this type of attitude "obstructs" the pipeline and is very harmful to organizations.

Transition 3: from managing managers to managing a role

This transition involves challenges that require the development of communication skills. Besides, chief operating officers need to manage some areas with which they are unfamiliar, so they must strive to understand and value them.

To be successful in this leadership transition also requires what the authors call "greater managerial maturity". In part, this means taking a broad, long-term perspective, especially applied to your role.

Transition 4: from operational manager to business manager

For any organization, this transition is crucial because business managers are responsible for financial results. In this leadership position, professionals have significant autonomy, which can be a benefit or a disadvantage for each individual - and it is up to the company to assess this individually when occupying the position.

Here there needs to be a big increase in skills, time management and work values. Business managers not only have to learn to run different roles, but They must also be able to work with people from various backgrounds. Therefore, they need to become more aware of diversity issues and be able to communicate effectively.

Transition 5: from business manager to group manager

While a business manager values his own business's success, a group manager values the others' business's success, inspires and supports those who report to him. The distinction is important because some people are only satisfied when they receive most of the merit.

Among the skills to be developed in this transition are strategy evaluation, development, and business managers evaluation. Besides, at this level, the leader must have a global perspective - think broadly and consider complexities when running multiple businesses.

Values test: do you know what is most important to you?

Transition 6: from group manager to company administrator

The transition to the sixth pass is much more focused on values than skills because these leaders (CEOs, for example) need to define a direction and develop operational mechanisms to know and drive performance that is in line with the long-term strategy. Deadline.

At this level, there is a shift from the focus of responsibility and strategic thinking to the visionary and the complete transition from an operational to a global perspective. Business leaders need to abandon concerns about "parts" (such as products and individual consumers) and focus on the whole.

CEOs who arrive at this passage having skipped one or more of the others can impair direct reports and individuals' performance throughout the chain. These problems in transition 6 occur, for the most part, for two reasons: it is difficult to develop a CEO, and leaders are not usually aware that this level requires a significant change in values.

Transition and political leadership

Photo by Paweł Czerwiński on Unsplash

Transition processes are extremely complex. On the one hand, there is the deconstruction of a delegitimized order, but which still has institutional power (financial resources and capacity for state coercion), and on the other, an attempt is made to institutionalize a new socially legitimate order. There is a disagreement between two points of view that can be resolved either violently or peacefully.

Managing these processes is a huge challenge for political leadership. Dismantling an undemocratic regime and, at the same time, laying the foundations for a new system of freedoms requires a set of specific and well-developed attributes (charisma, self-confidence, maturity and group management); Furthermore, it requires a context that facilitates political operation (incentives that stimulate support from followers and cooperation from the counterpart). For this reason, successful democratization processes are not usually guided by "one messianic leader" but by "several leaders" who share roles and cooperate.

The ability to implement reforms and change an authoritarian system is different from introducing new institutional practices that consolidate democracy. There are at least two types of leadership in peaceful transitions: transitional and transformational. The transitional leader comes from the decadent order and introduces reforms intending to sustain the system: more than a revolutionary, and he is a pragmatist with a desire to survive.

For his part, the transformational leader represents the new order: he expresses an alternative and radical vision of society.

To develop peaceful and institutional transitions, both leaders are vital because the process will be subject to strong political tensions: the conservatives want to stop the reforms, and radicals, speed them up. The institutional breakdown is avoided when the leaders of both groups cooperate and distribute tasks: the transitional leader persuades the representatives of the authoritarian system that "liberalization" is necessary to continue in the political game and the transformational leader convinces the radicals of that "democratization" has to be progressive and consensual.

The transitional leader

Photo by <u>Library of Congress</u> on <u>Unsplash</u>

It is tempting to interpret the democratic transition as an epic episode led by a "revolutionary leader" with extraordinary personal attributes. It is inspiring to hear narratives about great men shaping history with the power of their will. But the reality is less romantic, and, at times, democratizing events are initiated by political leaders of the authoritarian system, whose goal is to reform it, not dismantle it. This is precisely the basic characteristic of the transitional leader: he comes from the prevailing regime. He is not an upstart but an actor of tradition who knows and knows how to handle the system's power structure. He is not a convert but a faithful believer in the original political project; but it has a broad vision that allows it to anticipate the need to reform it, to guarantee its subsistence,

PERSONAL GROWTH QUESTIONS

1. What are the action plans to achieve your goals?
2. What do you understand by the word "from managing others to managing managers"?
3. What do you also understand by the word "from managing managers to managing a role"?
4. What do you understand by action plan?
5. How can you contribute to your personal growth towards The Resurrection IMPRINT Act.

Chapter Five

RESURRECTION LEADERS

Photo by Christine Sandu on Unsplash

According to the Gospel accounts, a party of women disciples went to Jesus' tomb, which was in the garden of Joseph of Arimathea, a Sanhedrin member and a secret disciple of Jesus. They found the tomb's stone moving and the tomb being vacant, and they told Peter and the other disciples that Jesus' body was not there. Later on, numerous disciples saw Jesus in Jerusalem, also entering a locked room; he was also seen in Galilee. (The positions and times of the appearances vary between Gospels.) The resurrected Lord's account wandering the Earth for 40 days and then rising into heaven is contained only in the book of Acts of the Apostles.

What does the resurrection of Jesus Christ mean?

Photo by Mateus Campos Felipe on Unsplash

For a variety of reasons, Jesus' resurrection is significant. For starters, the resurrection demonstrates God's colossal power. It is the same as believing in God to believe in the resurrection. God has the power to raise the dead if He exists and created and controls the world. Because He is so powerful, He is undeserving of our faith and worship. Only God, who created life, can resurrect it after death, reversing death's ugliness, and removing the sting and gaining victory over death (1 Corinthians 15:54–55). By raising Jesus from the dead, God reminds us of His complete dominion over life and death.

Jesus' resurrection is also important since it validates his claim to be the Son of God and Messiah. According to Jesus, the resurrection was a "sign from heaven" that validated His ministry (Matthew 16:1–4). Hundreds of eyewitnesses attest to Jesus Christ's resurrection, demonstrating beyond a shadow of a doubt that He is the world's Savior (1 Corinthians 15:3–8).

Jesus Christ's resurrection is significant because it demonstrates His sinless nature and divine existence. According to the Bible

(Psalm 16:10), God's "Holy One" will never see corruption, and Jesus never saw corruption, even after He died (Acts 13:32–37). "Through Jesus, remission of sins is proclaimed to you," Paul preached, "and everyone who believes in him is set free from all sin" (Acts 13:38–39).

The resurrection of Jesus Christ confirms His divinity and the Old Testament prophecies about His suffering and resurrection (see Acts 17:2–3). Christ's resurrection also supported His claims that He will be reborn on the third day (Mark 8:31; 9:31; 10:34). If Jesus Christ is not reborn, we have no hope of being resurrected. Without Christ's salvation, we have no Savior, no redemption, and no promise of eternal life. As Paul put it (1 Corinthians 15:14–19), our faith would be "useless," the gospel would be "powerless," and our sins would remain unforgivable.

"I am always the resurrection and the life," Jesus declared (John 11:25), claiming to be the source of both. There is no resurrection and no everlasting life without Christ. Jesus has no power over death because He is more than a provider of life; He is life. Jesus gives those who believe in Him the gift of life, allowing us to share in His triumph over death (1 John 5:11–12). Since we have overcome death by having the immortality Jesus gives, we who believe in Jesus Christ will experience rebirth. (1 Corinthians 15:53–57) Death has no hope of winning.

In other words, Jesus made it possible for people to live after they died. The resurrection of Jesus Christ is important because it confirms the Christian belief in the resurrection of humans. Unlike other religions, Christianity has a creator who promises that His followers will live forever. Any other religion was founded by men or prophets who were all doomed to die. As Christians, we believe that God became man, died for our sins, and rose from the dead on the third day. The cemetery couldn't hold him because he was too tall. He is alive and well today, sitting at the right hand of the Father in heaven (Hebrews 10:12).

The Bible guarantees that believers will be saved as Jesus Christ returns with His church at the rapture. Such assurance results in a great victorious song, as Paul writes in 1 Corinthians 15:55, "Where, O death, is your victory?" Where is your sting, death? Hosea 13:14 is a good example of this.

The importance of Christ's resurrection influences our new service to the Lord. Paul ends his resurrection discourse by saying, "Therefore, my dear brothers and sisters, stand firm." Allow yourself to be swayed by nothing. Sometimes devote your whole heart and soul to the Lord's work, trusting that your efforts will not be in vain" (1 Corinthians 15:58). We may face persecution and danger for the sake of Christ because we know that, like our Lord, we will be reborn to new life (verses 30–32). Throughout history, thousands of Christian martyrs have willingly given up their earthly lives in exchange for everlasting life and the promise of a resurrection resulting from Jesus Christ's resurrection.

For any believer, the resurrection is a victorious and glorious triumph. According to the Bible (1 Corinthians 15:3–4), Jesus Christ died, was buried, and rose on the third day. And He's already en route! What does the resurrection of Jesus Christ mean? It exemplifies who Jesus is. It demonstrates that God recognized Jesus' atonement for our sins. It reflects God's power to bring the dead back to life. It ensures that those who believe in Christ will have their bodies resurrected to eternal life rather than dying.

In Islam, the doctrine of the resurrection is also taught. Both men will die at Doomsday and then be resurrected from the dead. Second, each person will be judged based on his life's record, held in two books, one listing good deeds and the other listing evil deeds. Unbelievers will go to hell after the Judgment, while faithful Muslims will go to heaven, a place of peace and bliss.

It is a common practice in business schools and corporations to use movies to drive home lessons in Leadership. It's unusual to come across a film or a series demonstrating the various qualities and principles of a successful leader. Let us now turn to the critical lessons of Leadership that we can derive from the protagonist.

1.Establish a shared vision with your tribe (read your team or organization)

Your vision is very clear from the beginning: to free your tribe and religion from the clutches of the enemies and establish a state where he can hold the teachings of their faith sacred. He will not allow anything to stand between him and this vision, including his brethren. It allows him to establish clarity in the minds of his tribe and inspires them to the extent of sacrificing their lives to achieve their leader's vision.

2. It is all about your people

You make no mistake in selecting the team, which can help him achieve the vision. Without having the right people in the right seat, vision remains a dream, and equally important is to empower them. He puts complete faith and backs them to the hilt by assigning them critical missions all along his journey. He stands by their side in their need and fights for their lives.

3. Hire, Fire and communicate based on your value system

People prefer to work with a leader who is aware of their needs and beliefs and who lives by them. You have a well-developed value system that is the foundation of his vision, and he seizes every opportunity to articulate to the people who follow him. He hires (makes him his ally) and fires (exiles them or kills them) his team members purely on this value system.

4. Balance hard truths and optimism

Every decision we make will not result in success. We will encounter failures, but it is the factor of resilience that helps us bounce back into the game to win the more massive war.

You face several setbacks; there are times where his strategy fails, he is deceived by the traitors in his camp and falls prey to the state's politics, but he never allows himself to be wrecked. He makes the necessary adjustments to the strategy, plan of execution and gets back right into the game just in time to win. He does all this with a sense of eternal optimism without ignoring the facts.

5. Act Decisively

As a leader, once you decide, unless there's a good reason to change your focus, stick with it. You aim to move the company forward, but you won't do that if you can't make a firm decision.

With a big-picture view, you can balance emerging opportunities with his long-term goals and objectives. He makes the tough decision to migrate his tribe from one place to another and leaves behind his own family as they do not align with his vision. He never falls for the temptations of pleasures or short-term success.

6. Have an inclusive policy

If you advance in your career, you'll need

to establish confidence with your coworkers to influence others. Concentrate on learning about their motives and encouraging them to express themselves. You should then apply what you've learned to make a difference and demonstrate that their opinion counts. It's also about bringing gender, ethnicity, age, ability, and experience diversity to the team.

You can break several such barriers, win people's hearts in distant lands, different ethnic backgrounds, and make them part of his tribe.

7. Great leaders have a Mentor

Leadership is hard and lonely. Good things take a lot of time to accomplish. Attempting to complete them on your own is nearly impossible. That is why all successful leaders have mentors and teach others. Mentors challenge you by pushing out of your comfort zone, which leads to growth, they pray for your wellbeing, and they are your confidant to reduce stress.

That's why facts cannot justify the Resurrection.

We can still go to the Holy Sepulcher today, and what do we see? Nothing! We are faced with an absence, the only undue absence: we know that we are born by chance, we live we don't know how and we don't know how long, we are sure that we go back to the tomb and stay there. And He is not there.

The empty tomb breaks the only certainty that man has, the only memory. In Greek, the language of the Gospels, the word 'remembrance' and 'sepulcher' are the same word; 'death' also has the same root. The memory of death that man has is practically broken. But it is not enough that the tomb is empty; how can I meet the Risen One?

There is a way to go. Among other things, the sign of the encounter with the Risen One is a very simple thing. Already Nietzsche said it: "It is not true that Christ is risen. Otherwise, Christians would have another face". That is, the encounter with the Risen

One means to rise again. If you meet with the light, you have light; if you meet with fire, you burn; if you meet with the water, you are at least wet!

PERSONAL GROWTH QUESTIONS

1. What are the attributes of a resurrection leaders?
2. How can you establish a shared vision with your tribe?
3. What do you understand about the resurrection according to the gospel?

What does the resurrection of Jesus Christ mean?

Chapter Six

SERVANT LEADERSHIP

Leaders are responsible for inspiring and influencing the employees under their command to carry out excellent work daily to achieve extraordinary results for the business and all the other professionals who make up the organization.

In this sense, it is necessary for entrepreneurs and entrepreneurs to invest a lot in developing leaders in their businesses, because thus the chances of achieving permanent success increase significantly.

But what kind of leadership to invest in? Well, it all depends on the type of business you have and how your organizational processes work.

So that you can clarify this doubt a little, I will introduce you to servant leadership and its characteristics so that you can know it a little more and analyze if it fits your company or not. Follow me on this reading and check it out!

What is servant leadership?

The term servant leadership. However, this is an approach that people have used for centuries: it is a form of management in which the leader focuses on the needs of others, especially team members, before considering his own.

Companies that adopt server leadership within their organizational culture pay close attention to development environments and support structures that promote high levels of employee satisfaction. Also, the servant leader works to build a learning organization in which individuals are encouraged to grow and become increasingly valuable.

Important characteristics of a servant leadership

A server leader has his focus mainly on people. However, he does not leave the search for results aside. It is precisely why he invests so much in professionals because he knows that only through these is it possible to achieve goals and objectives assertively.

Continue reading this powerful content and check out the other characteristics of the server leader:

1. Empower and develop people

The servant-leader gives people responsibility for their actions in the workplace. Through training, he recognizes the talents and strengths of employees.

Besides, he must encourage employees in their actions and their personal growth, showing that they are not mere subordinates but unique individuals, fully capable of contributing to the company becoming increasingly successful in the market.

2. Humility

The leader must be humble to recognize that employees can have more knowledge and experience than he. By recognizing the limits of his knowledge, he encourages creating a learning environment in which the professionals under his command can learn from each other, regardless of hierarchical levels, thus developing through his strong willingness and the exchange of experiences in the work environment.

Besides, he is a type of leader who knows the exact moments when he needs the help of his employees in certain tasks to move forward. Thus, he demonstrates humility and recognizes that he does not have all the knowledge and skills and that growth is only possible if done in a group.

3. Authenticity

This is another significant factor, as it allows the servant leader to show employees that they can - and should - act according to their beliefs in the workplace.

To show his authenticity, the servant leader must act with integrity, fulfil what he promises, show consistency between what he does and what he says and be true to himself and the leadership principles he preaches.

4. Empathy

A servant leadership culture requires the ability to consider and experience the emotions and motivations of others. The servant-leader is understanding and empathetic towards those who work with him, whether they be members of his staff, colleagues, or superiors because he accepts them as individuals.

5. Targeting

Knowing exactly what the leader expects from each one is very important for employees and the organization. Therefore, it is necessary to offer guidance on what each one should do. This does not mean not giving freedom, but making it clear the expectations about each employee's work so that they know which way to go, even in an autonomous way.

6. Develop your leadership with Coaching

Coaching is one of the leadership developments processes that has helped professionals and companies achieve extraordinary results in an accelerated way. This is because, through the knowledge, techniques and tools it shares, the methodology empowers individuals to further improve their skills and abilities and become truly successful leaders.

EXAMPLES OF SERVANT LEADERSHIP

Martin Luther King, Jr. was a civil rights activist who was assassinated.

King did not always want to lead the Civil Rights Movement in the United States, but he recognized the need for equality. He was able to leave a positive legacy by putting other people's needs first, demonstrating that everyone can make a difference from a humble and serving mindset. Some of King's speeches still listen to daily because they are seen as having a ring of fact.

Nelson Mandela was a popular South African leader

Standing in front of his people, Mandela described himself as a humble servant with a deep love for his people and a desire to see them achieve equality. He would often take his speeches to the streets, putting his safety in jeopardy, and on other occasions, he would suffer harsh conditions in jail to get his message across.

Mother Teresa is a well-known figure.

As a result of her religion, Mother Teresa dedicated her life to helping others. As do most servant leaders, she had her critics, but no one could deny her motives for wanting to help others. Despite her emphasis on major changes and ability to share opinions that others would be hesitant to express, she never sought personal recognition. Many people regard her as a saint, and her life is regarded as a miracle.

AT THE TIME OF COVID-19, LEADERSHIP

During this pandemic time, we are watching with trepidation as our leaders attempt to control the spread of the disease and address an unprecedented emergency in a more or less orderly and careful manner.

We don't know when this health crisis will

end or what the consequences will be, but one thing is certain: some politicians will have proven to be more capable than others of dealing with the crisis and minimizing the harm to the communities they belong to.

It is precisely in the hardest periods that the devastating effects of inadequate leadership are highlighted and amplified: incompetence, arrogance, dishonesty, indifference to the suffering of others are, even more so in times of crisis, the detonators of social and economic upheaval.

The leaders who prove to be the most capable will be able to express qualities such as competence, humility, integrity, courage, and empathy and emotional intelligence.

Never as today, when the entire world population is exposed in all its vulnerability to fear and to suffer, the leadership of a country (and any other organized group) requires leaders to give trust and reassurance, connecting people in their emotions and values.

1. The most capable leaders: competent and empathic

Why do so many inept men become leaders (and what can be done about it)" Some personality characteristics, such as egocentrism, complacency, and an excessive belief in one's abilities, have been mistakenly interpreted as signs of a strong and charismatic personality, rather than being considered warning signs of personality disorders, as they should be.

Excessive optimism is often confused with competence.

Consequently, we have a plethora of incompetents (and narcissists) in corporate leadership roles. Institutions, and nations.

This phenomenon can escalate and intensify during times of crisis when the "powerful man in charge" seems to be the panacea for all ills.

Leaders who are selfish and self-centered instill fear, distrust, and anger in their communities, wreaking havoc not just on the environment and social cohesion but also on productivity.

On the other hand, positive and beneficial leadership is a valuable resource for societies and organizations, improving morale and success.

Concerning other more critical dimensions of leadership: knowledge and technical competence, intellect, modesty, dedication, networking, honesty, and empathy, self-confidence and the strenuous pursuit of personal achievement even at the cost of the common good must be set aside.

It's competence's retaliation for improvisation, the superficiality and banality of appearance.

Competence and discipline, however, are insufficient. At the same time, it's important to take a more empathic, human approach, even if it's counter-intuitive, because only in this way can we be inspired to develop a taste for creativity, insight, diversity, and inclusion, and, above all, we'll be empowered to follow ambitious goals, even if it means making compromises and renunciations.

The winning leader is the one who can lead a group (whether it's a group of individuals or a business team) to mutual success by intercepting, understanding, and giving voice to people's thoughts, emotions, and moods, and putting personal interests aside in favour of the community's overall well-being.

Emotional intelligence and empathy are critical in this regard, and women, who have a natural propensity for these skills more often than men, will undoubtedly be able to make a significant and decisive contribution to the hoped-for cultural change if they are allowed to reach decision-making positions more frequently than they have been so far.

2. **Generosity's advantages**

If constructive and sharing, cooperative and supportive group mechanisms are activated, the uncertainties and problems created by the current emergency can be better handled.

Givers is people who choose to give rather than take; they are generous with their time, resources, expertise, talents, ideas, and connections.

They have a deep sense of duty for others around them and a predisposition to behave in the best interests of others. They enjoy contributing without expecting much in return, and they are willing to put the group's interests ahead of their own.

They communicate in a relaxed and participatory manner (Powerless), and they often use the first-person plural (we, our...) in conversation.

On the other hand, Takers often put their interests first, taking more than they offer and draining others' wealth and energy.

They are often based on themselves, have a hyper-competitive attitude, believe they are superior to others, and overestimate their achievement while underestimating that of others.

Their reference values are economic prosperity, strength, and abuse of the opponent in a win-lose logic.

They come at a price and pose a significant threat to social stability.

Matchers, who make up most of the population (roughly 60%), seek a balance of giving and take, can support others in return for benefits, base relationships on equal favors transactions, and defend themselves with reciprocity.

They approach relationships with others respectfully and collaboratively, driven by the concept of fair play. However, since they are often looking for a reward in return for their assistance, they are less successful than Givers at positively impacting those around them.

The law in cultures controlled by taker principles takes as much as possible from others while adding as little as possible. You only support others when you are persuaded that the personal benefits outweigh the costs, and you are afraid that you will be seen as poor by doing so.

By discouraging mutual helping and contributing activities, this strategy invariably leads to rivalry and internal conflict.

The standard of "matching cultures" assists those who assist us, maintaining a constant balance of giving and take. While cultures dominated by matchers' values benefit from a more collaborative atmosphere than cultures dominated by takers' values, they are still inefficient environments for cooperation, sharing, and creating new ideas and information that emerge from cross-fertilization.

The Givers have a stronger capacity for productive contact with others and can foster a more accessible, supportive atmosphere focused on confidence and harmony.

People in giving cultures freely assist others without asking anything in return.

From a variety of perspectives, this supportive and supportive activity increases the efficacy of unified communities:

It improves community cohesion and coordination.

It creates an atmosphere more conducive to compliance, so people feel that their interests are truly top priority.

It promotes the dissemination and sharing of information, as well as the transfer of know-how and skills.

Numerous studies have shown that compassion improves the physical and emotional well-being of both those who receive it and those who give it, increases energy levels, strengthens a sense of belonging to the community to which they belong, and encourages teamwork.

3. FINAL THOUGHTS

The future presents us with numerous and daunting challenges. Nothing would be the same, and we must be willing to accept new paradigms.

For starters, a more transparent and confident attitude toward emerging innovations has proven invaluable in reducing the negative effects of alienation and inactivity while also promoting the social and economic fabric's stability.

In this situation, a fundamental transformation of nations' and organizations' leadership and command models, characterized by empathy, compassion, hospitality, unity, and a willingness to listen and support others, appears critical.

Leaders will need to show the ability to listen and "see" people, get in touch with them, understand feelings, and make decisions that maximize the common good to rebuild a more just and equal society.

PERSONAL GROWTH QUESTIONS

1. How can you describe servant leadership?
2. characteristics of a servant leadership?
3. Who are the famous sample of servant leadership?
4. What are the role of leadership during pandemic time?

Chapter Seven

CONFLICT MANAGEMENT: HOW TO ADDRESS DIFFICULT SITUATIONS

Conflict can be defined as a divergence in which each of the actors involved wants to impose their point of view without making concessions to the other. It is a discrepancy between what a person desires and what hinders or prevents the satisfaction of that desire.

Can you tell me some synonyms for "conflict"?

"Clash", "war", "violence", "aggression", "controversy" are the terms closest to the meaning of this word considered negative.

You will certainly not have come up with words like "growth", "confrontation", "opportunity", or "collaboration". Too bad, because it is in the most difficult situations that the best opportunities arise.

Conflicts are inevitable in any context of daily life, so you need to recognize, manage and resolve them in a positive way. It is important to see them as an expression of different visions and moments of individual growth or possibly improve one's relationships through more effective communication.

"There is no progress without conflict: this is the law that civilization has followed to this day."

Correct conflict management is crucial in the private sphere, linked to family, friendship and love, and in the workplace, the scene of numerous crashes due to forced coexistence between subjects who do not know each other.

One of the rules of the fundamental rules is to remember that neither losers nor winners must emerge from a resolved conflict, but people who are satisfied with having found a meeting point.

Here are several pointers to help you keep

your relationships with others intact by preventing unnecessary misunderstandings:

- You have to consider the interests of all the actors involved;
- You have to consider the people separately from the problem;
- The solution must be acceptable to both parties;
- The majority must share the decision.

What can our reactions be during a conflict?

ABANDONMENT OR ELUSION Low assertiveness / low cooperation

This attitude expresses fear, weakness and low self-esteem. It is used when you want to postpone one problem or not put the other in difficulty.

ADVANTAGES: it is a way to calm the waters quickly. If the conflict is not very heated, it will eventually subside by itself.

DISADVANTAGES: the conflict can explode when you least expect it, so you will not be able to control the situation; you will also miss the opportunity to clarify the problem once and for all.

Complacency

Low assertiveness / high cooperation

In this case, we try to find a solution that suits both of us, containing and controlling emotions to preserve human relationships.

ADVANTAGES: it is a fast method that expresses willingness to listen to the proposals of others, hoping for a subsequent negotiation; it does not cause an escalation of violence due to a lack of taxation.

Others could ignore DISADVANTAGES: those who do not express their ideas in the search for solutions;

COMPROMISE

Moderate assertiveness / moderate cooperation

The contenders, although both come out as "winners", sin on the human relationship.

ADVANTAGES: Both parties play an active role in the conversation and are quite satisfied with the outcome. It is the first step towards cooperation.

DISADVANTAGES: it could cause resentment and the desire to bully, putting the cooperation process in difficulty. It depends on the trust and availability of both parties, so it is not always possible. Takes time.

COMPARISON and COLLABORATION

High assertiveness / high cooperation

The two contenders express their points of view and are committed to finding a just solution. They don't want to fight, but they want to overcome the conflict.

ADVANTAGES: brings maximum satisfaction for both parties; expresses listening and respect, both for the other and for oneself; allows you to play an active role in negotiation.

DISADVANTAGES: it needs a lot of time and the availability and trust of both, so it is not always easy to hire; it requires a good knowledge of oneself and the other, and good communication skills.

FORCING

High assertiveness / low cooperation

Those who act in this way want to assert themselves over the other, laying the foundations for a real competition.

ADVANTAGES: it is implemented when you have little time available, you have the certainty of being right, you want to get an immediate result, you are not afraid that interpersonal relationships will be compromised. Those who impose themselves have strong self-esteem.

DISADVANTAGES: if you impose yourself frequently, sooner or later, you risk isolation; the imposition does not enrich you internally because it does not involve a listening phase. You also risk raising criticisms from your interlocutors.

Conflict Management

The elements to be considered in conflict management can be summarized in the so-called SPACE model:

"S" stands for "self."

"P" stands for "purpose."

"A" stands for "audience."

"C" stands for "code."

"E" stands for "experience."

The self-analyses specifically: who we are, who the subjects involved, and the assumptions made by these subjects. Also, we need to better understand how roles can affect us.

Purpose, that is, it is necessary to clarify the mutual objectives. Sometimes, for example, personal goals overlap with corporate ones, generating opportunities for conflict and misunderstandings.

The objectives must be expressed positively;

- They must be under the responsibility of whoever defines them;
- They must be measurable;
- They must be shared;
- They must be consistent with both the company's values and personal ones;

The audience, who is involved besides the protagonists? How do the bonds that these subjects have on the protagonists of the conflict impact? Were they involved from the beginning or during construction? Do we know their role? What contribution did they make to the conflict situation? Did they help overcome it?

Experience, considering the personal history and the situational aspects that the subjects bring with them during the discussion, to identify the resources necessary for conflict management. Here are some things to consider:

Vision and values;

Relations;

Focus;

Motivation;

Creativity / innovation;

Methods, material, time, space;

Problem Solving: 5 Steps to Overcoming Conflicts

Conflicts make you uncomfortable, and you usually try to avoid them, but would you like to learn to react differently? Many conflict situations arise in your company every day, and would you like to intervene to improve the general climate? Are you looking for useful tools to manage conflicts in the family and the workplace? Do your friends have an aggressive attitude, and are you afraid that they will cause conflicts at any moment?

Rest assured, there is an established method that will help you in resolving the most difficult conflicts.

Have you ever heard of "Problem Solving"?

It is a cognitive process that allows you to analyze a given situation and make assumptions about the best way to go when faced with a problem.

It is an activity that man has always practiced for his survival, from the invention of the wheel to the control of fire and the first systems to cultivate the land. Over time, real techniques have been developed to solve the most disparate problems, from the scientific and economic ones to the emotional and relational ones.

Whatever your problem is, you can use this very flexible model based on six steps:

1. Identify and define the problem

Before reaching the solution, you need to invest time and energy to better understand the problem in terms of needs, fears and feelings. A problem is a "gap" between the current state and the desired one, that is, a leap between where you are now and where you would like to arrive. To define a problem, you can compare your current situation with the hypothetical one of the futures through a gap analysis.

2. Consider all possible solutions

Devote yourself to the creative production of ideas to transform the problem situation into an optimal, or at least acceptable, situation for all stakeholders. To find more solutions to the problem, you can help you through some Brainstorming sessions.

3. Choose the best solution

Now that you have identified several possible solutions, it is time to select the most valid one. Evaluate all the options and eliminate, one by one, the ones you deem less appropriate. You could analyze every possible solution that comes to your mind based on its effectiveness, time, cost and effort required.

4. Create an action plan

At this stage, determine the actual steps to take. You can also create a plan B in case unexpected circumstances arise. The famous

"5W Rule" - who, what, where, when and why - will help you get to the heart of the problem more quickly and effectively.

5. Take action!

You can't be a good problem solver if you don't take action. Sometimes our actions may involve risks, but this is inevitably part of the game. No one comes to success right away without ever having experienced some failure.

Conclusion

When a conflict is dealt with incorrectly, by resorting to force, abandonment or forcing (as we have seen previously), it can lead to resentment, resentment, indifference or at worst irreparable breakdowns. However, when done correctly, it can boost levels of comprehension, increase interlocutor's feelings of confidence, and reinforce bonds.

PERSONAL GROWTH QUESTIONS

1. What is Conflict Management?
2.   What can our reactions be during a conflict?
3. What are the **Steps take to Overcoming Conflicts?**

Afterword Thoughts From a Wise Leader

Leadership phrases

As a result, for a leader to be deemed effective, he must fulfil specific roles. However, the debate about Leadership does not stop here, as we aim to illustrate how some academics and thinkers view the leader's figure. And, of course, these leadership phrases can motivate you. Look into:

"Incredible leaders go out of their way to improve their team's self-esteem. If people believe in them, it's amazing what they can achieve." Sam Walton

"It's not about names, roles, or hierarchies when it comes to Leadership. It is a life that affects others." John C. Maxwell

"Hire character, train skills." Peter Schutz

"No man will be a great leader if he wants to do everything himself or if he wants to take all the credit for doing so." Andrew Carnegie

"Good Leadership. It is not a formula or program, and it is a human activity that comes from the heart and takes into account the hearts of other people. It is an attitude, not a routine." Lance Secretan

"If your actions inspire others to think more, learn more, do more, and grow stronger, you are a leader." John Quincy Adams is a well-known politician in the United States.

"Innovation sets a leader apart from a follower." Steve Jobs is a well-known American entrepreneur

"Leadership is a mindset, a way of acting, and, most importantly, a way of thinking, communicating," says the author. Simon Sinek is a best-selling author and motivational speaker.

"Leadership is determined by performance, not attributes; effective Leadership is not about speaking or being loved." Drucker, Peter

"Taking responsibility, not making excuses, is what leadership is all about." Mitt

Romney is a Republican presidential candidate.

"Most important quality for a leader is unquestionably integrity. It is impossible to achieve success without it. Eisenhower, Dwight D.

"A true leader doesn't need to lead; he's content to point the way." Miller, Henry

"Influence, not authority, is the secret to effective leadership." Blanchard, Kenneth H.

"A leader who does not think twice about taking his country into combat is unfit to rule." Golda Meir is a well-known Israeli politician.

"Recognize that everybody has gifts and skills is one of the keys to Leadership. A good leader will learn to collect these virtues for the same purpose." Benjamin Carson

"Without a vision or a goal, a person cannot manage his own life, let alone the lives of others." Jack Weatherford

"Leadership is the ability to turn the vision into reality." Warren Bennis

DISCUSSION QUESTIONS

1. What is leadership?
2. What is autocratic, situational, democratic, liberal   a transformational leadership?
3. What are the attributes to develop an organizational leadership?
4. Characteristics of a good leader?
5. What are seven tried-and-true methods for moving from decision to action?
6. Ancient Chinese proverb states that twenty years was the perfect time to plant a tree, what do you understand by this statement?
7. How can you quit second-guessing the decisions?
8. What are the things possible distraction can lead to while moving from decision into action?
9. How can you build a community that resists any situation?
10. What are the action plans to achieve your goals?

11. What do you understand by the word "from managing others to managing managers"?

12. What do you also understand by the word "from managing managers to managing a role"?

13. What are the attributes of a resurrection leaders?

REFERENCES

Fast Company. 2021. *7 Ways To Identify Leaders Among Your Employees*. [online] Available at: <https://www.fastcompany.com/3044953/7-ways-to-identify-leaders-among-your-employees> [Accessed 22 April 2021].

Sand, M., 2005. *How to manage an effective nonprofit organization*. Franklin Lakes, NJ: Career Press.

7 Ways To Identify Leaders Among Your Employees. (2021). Retrieved 22 April 2021, from https://www.fastcompany.com/3044953/7-ways-to-identify-leaders-among-your-employees

Edberg, H. (2021). How to Take Action: 12 Habits that Turn Dreams into Reality. Retrieved 22 April 2021, from https://www.positivityblog.com/how-to-take-action/

Sand, M. (2005). *How to manage an effective nonprofit organization*. Franklin Lakes, NJ: Career Press.

How to Create a Professional Learning Community. (2021). Retrieved 22 April 2021, from https://www.edutopia.org/professional-learning-communities-collaboration-how-to

Peaceful Transitions. (2021). Retrieved 22 April 2021, from https://peaceful-transitions.com/

Resurrection Leadership: A Different Kind of Leadership Skill-Set | MBO Partners. (2021).

Retrieved 22 April 2021, from
https://www.mbopartners.com/mbo-
advantage/consulting-quarterly/resurrection-
leadership/

Servant Leadership: A bibliometric Review.
(2020). *International Journal Of Organizational Leadership*.
doi: 10.33844/ijol.2020.60501

Resolving Conflict Situations | People & Culture.
(2021). Retrieved 22 April 2021, from
https://hr.berkeley.edu/hr-network/central-guide-
managing-hr/managing-
hr/interaction/conflict/resolving

Made in the USA
Columbia, SC
02 September 2021

44679774R00153